Landmark Visito

Madeira

Richard Sale

Published by
Landmark Publishing
Ashbourne Hall, Cokayne Ave, Ashbourne,
Derbyshire DE6 1EJ England

Contents

Welcome to Madeira	**6**
History	8
Madeira today	13
Geography	14
Food & Drink	16
Flora & Fauna	20
Madeiran costume	21
Festivals & Events	24
1. Funchal	**26**
Walking Tour 1	31
Madeira Wine	35
Waling Tour 2	43
Walking Tour 3	48
Walking Tour 4	53
Madeiran Embroidery	54
Places to Visit	60
2. Around Funchal	**62**
Quinta do Palheiro Ferreiro	64
Monte	65
Curral das Freiras	72
Places to Visit	73
3. The Western Island	**74**
Funchal to Porto Moniz	76
Porto Moniz to Calheta	77
Calheta to Ponta do Sol	78
Ponta do Sol to Ribeira Braua	79
Ponta do Sol to Funchal	80
Place to Visit	81
4. Central Madeira	**82**
Funchal to Faial	83
Pico de Arieiro	83
Santana	85
Santana to São Vicente	86
A detour to Seixal & Porto Moniz	88
São Vicente to Encumeada	90
Encumeada to Funchal	90
Places to Visit	93
5. The Eastern Island	**94**
Funchal to Santa Cruz	95
Santa Cruz	96
Machuco	100
Ponta de São Lourenço	104
Machico to Funchal: the inland route	105
Places to Visit	108
6. Porto Santo & The Desertas	**110**
Porto Santo	111
Vila Baleira	114
7. Walking on Madeira	**122**
A selection of walks	128
Ponta da São Lourenço	128
Pico de Arieiro & Pico Ruivo	129
Rabaçal	130
Levada dos Tornos	131
Eira do Serrado Curral	132
Levada da Central da Ribeira da Janela	132
Levada da Serra do Faial	133
Santana to São Jorge	134
Pico Ruivo to Encumeada	135
Levada do Caldeirão Verde	136
Ribeiro Frio: Levada do Furado	137
Bica da Cana: Levada do Serra	138
Guided Walks	139
FactFile	**140**
Banks, Credit Cards & Currency	140
Camping	140

Children	140	Disabled Visitors	147
Climate	141	Electricity	147
Restaurants	142	Emergencies	148
Western Madeira	142	Health Care	148
Central Madeira	142	Language	148
Eastern Madeira	143	National Holidays	148
Restaurants in Funchal	144	Newspapers	149
Nightlife	145	Pharmacies	149
Bars	146	Post & Telephone Services	149
Theatre/Music/Cinema	146	Sport	149
Casino	146	Time	153
Shops	146	Tipping	153
Consulates	147	Tourist Information Offices	153
Customs & Entry Regulations	147	Travel	155

Welcome to
Madeira

Opposite: Antigos Areeiro

The Island of Flowers, the Pearl of the Atlantic, the Isle of Eternal Spring - these are just a few of the names that, over the years, Madeira has acquired from those captivated by its beauty. Close to Africa, yet part of Europe, the island mixes the two, creating something exotic but sophisticated, the ideal holiday combination.

Top Tips

Quinta das Cruzes - Madeira means orchids and there is nowhere better to see them than the grounds of this delightful mansion/museum.

Mercado dos Lavradores - Funchal's Market Hall is an assault on the senses. Go early to see the exotic fish or later to enjoy the flower sellers.

Monte - In a world of theme parks and video games the Monte toboggan ride might seem a bit tame. But the ride has its moments and is pure delight.

Curral das Freiras - The view down to this magically set village is breathtaking.

Pico de Arieiro - Even non-walkers should follow the road to the car park close to the highest island volcano. Better still, follow the path across a landscape as different from the coastal lushness as could be imagined.

Porto Moniz - Despite a recent upsurge in visitors, this little port, remote from Funchal and the airport, still retains its old-world charm.

Porto Santo - For genuine peace and tranquility, this off-shore island is hard to beat.

Porta de São Lourenço - Where jagged volcanic rock meets an uncompromising ocean.

Camacha - Wicker capital of the island.

A Levada Walk - Even committed non-walkers should follow one levada. Levada do Risco at Rabaçal is short and reaches a splendid waterfall.

The island has a truly enviable climate, its temperature fixed in a narrow range that means overcoats can be left behind, but the occasionally overpowering heat of nearby Africa never troubles. The volcanic origins of the island have left a high, jagged interior which attracts clouds and rain, the rain watering a fertile volcanic soil which, with the ever-present sun, produces textbook conditions for plant growth. The Island of Flowers is an appropriate name - Madeira's gardens are its great joy as the annual Flower Festival makes amply clear. Garden lovers will find more than enough to satisfy them, and will also find that away from the formal gardens, where the orchids that are the island's speciality bloom, Madeira is alive with colour at all times of the year: if there is a an uncultivated patch of earth it will soon be colonised by an exotic flower.

Madeira: The Name

A Genoese chart, dating from 1351 and now in the Laurentian Library in Florence, shows Madeira, calling it the Isola di Lolegname. The name is believed to derive from the Arabic el agham, wood, and this is very likely as the Arabic traders of north-west Africa almost certainly knew of the island's existence.

When Zarco re-discovered the island, he too was impressed by the fact that it was tree-covered, and called it Ilhéu da Madeira, madeira being Portuguese for wood.

The island's rugged heartland offers a contrast to the coast where the gardens are found. Here angular peaks provide their own beauty, though the less intimidating and sheltered slopes are still a paradise for the plant lover. This is country for the mountain walker. But Madeira has one final secret: the rain that falls on the highlands is piped in water channels hewn from the bare rock - levadas, hollowed out in medieval times - and taken to the coast where it irrigates the land. Paths were built beside these water channels so that they could be readily inspected, and these paths offer walkers of modest pretensions the chance to explore the island's centre. Occasionally the paths are exposed, but they are always clear: the fear of getting lost in a strange land is eliminated.

Some historians believe that Madeira is the source of the legend of Atlantis, the fabled land that lay beyond Gibraltar. It may not have the beaches of the Mediterranean Europe, or even of the Canaries to the south, but it has so much more. It may not have been Atlantis, but it is an island on which stories of legendary holidays can easily take root.

History

Legend has it that in 1344 a minor English nobleman called Robert Machin, eloping with his true love Anna d'Arfet - whose hand had been promised by her father to a man of nobler standing - was in a ship which a storm forced on to (or even shipwrecked on) the eastern shore of Madeira. There are various versions of the story, but all of them have Anna dying soon after. Some versions have her death following the heartbreak of the pair being abandoned by the crew of the refloated ship. Other versions have both Robert and Anna dying and being buried by the crew. All legends agree that there was a further shipwreck, either of the crew on the Moroccan coast, or of Robert when he escaped Madeira on a home-made raft. But all versions agree that from the stories told to the Moroccans word of Madeira's existence filtered back to Lisbon.

Whether the legend is true of not - and there is evidence to support it: it is said that on the first 'official' landing on the island the grave of Anna d'Arfet was found, and the island certainly appears on charts which pre-date the official discovery - Madeira's recorded history dates from 1418 when an expedition financed by Henry the Navigator, Prince of Portugal, was blown out into the Atlantic while exploring the coast of Africa. The leaders of the expedition was João Gonçalves who had taken the extra surname Zarco, making light of the fact that it was a nickname, referring to the squint in one eye. Zarco had a co-leader, Tristão Vaz Teixeira, and the pair landed first on Porto Santo, from where the island of Madeira was visible, though it was not until an expedition was mounted two years later that the two men, and Bartolomeo Perestrelo, landed on Madeira, near to what is now Machico on the eastern shore. The men claimed the islands for Portugal and were given the governorships. Perestrelo received Porto Santo, the two co-leaders dividing Madeira between them.

The division was curious, being along a diagonal line from the north-west to south-east tips of the island. João Gonçalves Zarco governed south-western Madeira from Funchal, while Tristão Vaz Teixeira governed the north-east from Machico. The three men ran their parts of the island (or in Perestrelo's case the whole of his island) as personal kingdoms: although the Portuguese king maintained sovereign rights, and levied taxes, on the islands, it was left to the governors to parcel out land to settlers of their choosing and to police and administer justice. Not until 1495 when Manuel I ascended to the throne of Portugal did the islands become officially crown property. From that date onwards, Madeira has been a part of Portugal.

Prosperity & decline

By 1495 the prosperity of Madeira had grown dramatically. Although the early history of the island is usually claimed to have been one of a developing sugar industry, the first settlers largely farmed cereals, the island's soil producing ten times as much grain as the same area on the mainland. But this first economic boom was not sustained by cereals, the money being ploughed back into the land in the form of sugar plantations. It is thought that the first slaves, from Africa and the Canaries, arrived in 1452. Within twenty years Madeira was the major sugar producer for Europe, its wealth bringing ambitious merchants from the mainland. One of these was Christopher Columbus who, as we shall see at Porto Santo, may even have planned his great voyage of discovery on the island.

Madeira

Taking in the view, Areeiro

Windsurfing, Costa Leste

10

Welcome to Madeira

Madeira

Porto Da Cruz

11

The sugar boom lasted almost a century: by 1500 only Lisbon and Porto were greater Portuguese cities than Funchal. But by 1525 competition from the sugar plantations of the New World caused Madeira's prosperity began to decline. It is ironical that it was after the decline that the island was attacked, in 1566, by Bertrand de Montluc a French pirate. As with all coastal cities in Europe, Madeira's main towns had been repeatedly attacked during the late fifteenth and early sixteenth centuries. Funchal had begun to build a defensive wall and fortress, but the failure of the sugar trade had meant it was inadequate. De Montluc's raid was the most serious of these attacks, his men killing several hundred Madeirans, ransacking houses and churches for their treasure and destroying everything they could not haul back to their ships, including countless barrels of wine from the fledgling wine industry. The pirates were on the island for over two weeks, but by the time a fleet arrived from Lisbon they had set sail for the Canaries.

Spain

Madeira was slow to recover, and Portugal itself was in a parlous state, a disastrous war against Morocco having emptied its exchequer. In 1580, a crisis arose over succession to the Portuguese throne. Philip II of Spain claimed the throne and Portugal became part of Spain. The Spaniards united the two halves of Madeira (which had remained under separate governors despite the island having been taken over as crown property almost a century before) and improved the defences of Funchal. But,

seeing the Madeiran wine trade as a threat to their own, they reduced the size of vineyards and effectively eliminated wine exports. Sugar continued to provide some prosperity, but to this was added the export of wood.

Madeira had been heavily afforested when first settled, but slash-and-burn farming had reduced the size of the forests. Legend has it that a fire started soon after the first settlers arrived spread with such ferocity that it was still burning seven years later. Though the wood ash from the fires fertilised the soil, huge swathes of woodland were lost. Now the Spaniards took much of what remained: most of the ships of the Spanish Armada are said to have been made from Madeiran timber.

While Madeira was Spanish it was subject to repeated raids by English pirates, but after Portugal regained its independence in 1640 - a largely bloodless liberation at first, the Spanish crown being distracted by domestic problems and failing to challenge the Duke of Braganza when he declared himself King João IV - the English became Portugal's main ally. The restored English king, Charles II, married Catherine of Braganza in 1662, sealing an alliance with Portugal which has remained intact from that date, making it the oldest alliance in Europe. In 1659 the Portuguese had defeated a Spanish army at the battle of Elvas: Spain was now at war with England and France, and despite occasional Spanish attempts to re-establish control over Portugal, another Portuguese victory in 1665 forced Spain to reconsider. Finally, in 1668, almost 30 years after de facto independence, Spain accepted that

Portugal was a sovereign state.

Once again, Portuguese

In the wake of Anglo-Portuguese alliance, some English merchants had arrived in Madeira. Then in 1665, when Charles II banned the export of non-British goods to the new English colonies in North America, but exempted Madeira from the ban, English merchants now arrived in force, virtually taking over the island. In 1703 the Methuen Treaty between the two countries gave England a monopoly of the Madeiran Wine trade, one which they exploited to the full.

At this time slavery was still the main form of labour on the island. The Portuguese had always been rather better masters than the English or Spanish (if such distinctions can be made in so odious a trade) allowing slaves to be freed on the death of their masters. The slaves had not only been African, but also Moorish, and the influence of the latter is apparent throughout the island. It is seen in the architecture and most particularly in the network of levadas, the famous Madeiran water channels which bring water from the mountains - where it falls in cascades - to the arid terraces of the coastal strip. Slavery was abolished on Madeira earlier than in British colonies (trading was banned here in 1761, slavery itself was banned in 1775). The effect on the wine trade was limited, but that was not true of the Napoleonic Wars which followed soon after abolition.

When Napoleon failed to persuade Portugal to assist in a naval blockade of Britain, he invaded. Britain evacuated the Portuguese royal family and sent a force to protect Madeira. In a final irony, the ship taking Napoleon into exile called at Madeira in 1815 and took some Madeiran wine on board. Some of the British soldiers who were stationed on the island during the war stayed on after, further strengthening the 'Britishness' of Madeira. British - and then other nation's - tourists began to arrive, but the wine trade remained the major industry.

In 1852 mildew attacked the vines, a disaster which coincided with an outbreak of cholera that killed 7,000 islanders. Mildew resistant vines were imported from America, but they brought phylloxera which, in 1872, devastated the vines. The Madeira wine industry never fully recovered from these two blows and the effect on the island's economy was severe. The poverty was alleviated, to an extend, by the introduction of embroidery as a cottage industry: embroidery remains one of Madeira's main crafts. But the main change was the replacement of vines with bananas, the fruit being the mainstay of the island's economy until the tourist boom of the late twentieth century.

20th Century

In 1916, at the request of the British, Portugal blockaded some German ships in Lisbon harbour and confiscated all German possessions. The Germans retaliated by declaring war on Portugal. A U-boat was sent to Madeira, sinking a French warship in Funchal harbour and surfacing to shell the city. The shelling was repeated in 1917. Following the war, prohibition in American hit the

Carnival of courtship

The Madeirans

The early settlers of Madeira were, of course, Portuguese, but the wealth of the sugar trade soon brought entrepreneurs from Italy - Christopher Columbus was Italian - Spain and Holland. The sugar trade was based on slavery, and Africans and Canary Islanders were brought to satisfy the demand. Later Moors - North African Arabs - were also brought to the island. Then, when the wine trade replaced sugar as Madeira's wealth creator, the British arrived. When the Napoleonic Wars threatened Madeira the island was garrisoned with British soldiers, many of whom stayed when peace was restored to Europe. This remarkable mix of races has produced a Madeiran population whose characteristics range from blue-eyed and fair-haired through to those with dark skins and black hair, as diverse a range as can be found in so small an area anywhere in Europe.

Though today's Madeirans have such a range of origins, the island's language is Portuguese, with very few words added from other languages. Only the British have maintained their own language, the British 'merchant class' still taking English - though the descendants of the British Napoleonic soldiers have left no trace of the language.

The Madeirans are almost exclusively Catholic, the village folk tending - as elsewhere - to be the most devout.

Welcome to Madeira

Atlantic festival

faltering wine industry and then world recession caused Madeira's economy to stall. The same problems engulfed the mainland and in 1926 a military coup brought António de Oliveira Salazar to power. He remained in power until 1968 when a stroke caused his departure from office. The early Salazar years were harsh on Madeira. There were hunger riots in 1931, the rioters declaring themselves in favour of independence from Portugal. Troops were sent from the mainland to restore order and the leaders of the independence movement were imprisoned.

In 1974 after a bloodless coup (known as the Carnation Revolution because the soldiers involved pushed flowers down their gun barrels) overthrew Salazar's successor. In the wake of the revolution Madeira again sought independence. The attempt failed, but in 1976 Madeira was granted the status of an autonomous region within Portugal.

By 1974 tourism had grown dramatically, and the era of relative prosperity which followed quelled the cry for independence. In 1986 Portugal became a member of what is now the European Union. Membership has helped both the mainland and Madeira, and though there is still acute poverty in areas of the island, there is a hope that European monetary union, and increased tourism, will raise the living standards of all the islanders.

Madeira Today

The Região Autónoma de Madeira (the Autonomous Region of Madeira, invariably referred to by its initials - RAM) is governed by a 50 seat par-

The Statistics

Madeira is 60km (37.5 miles) long and 24km (15 miles) wide at its widest point.

Porto Santo, which lies 40km (25 miles) to the north-east, is 16km (10 miles) long and 5km (3 miles) wide at its widest point.

Madeira covers an area of 740 sq km (290 sq miles), Porto Santo an area of 45 sq kms (18 sq miles).

Madeira has a population of 280,000 of whom about half live in the capital, Funchal.

Porto Santo has a population of 4,000

Madeira is about 1,200 km (750 miles) south-west of Lisbon. It lies about 800 km (500 miles) from the African (Moroccan) coast and about 550 km (350 miles) north of the Canary Islands.

Madeira's highest mountain is Pico Ruivo at 1,862m (6,107ft).

liament which has been headed by Dr Alberto João Jardim, the popular leader of the PSD (Popular Social Democrat) party, since autonomy was granted in 1976. The RAM years have brought significant improvements in the quality of life of poorer Madeirans - though dreadful poverty is still a fact of island life - with electricity and roads having reached almost all villages and most now having schools and health clinics. But the problems facing the Madeiran government are difficult. The seas around the island, deep seas not amenable to modern fishing techniques have been, despite this, chronically over-fished. The work is also hard and dangerous, unappealing to many of the island's youth. They are no more attracted to agriculture, where the terraced fields are only farmed with great physical effort, the use of machinery being almost impossible.

Tourism offers a way forward, but the lack of beaches means that package holidays - which bring in lots of cash as well as importing rather less agreeable side-effects - are limited. Many who visit the island, returning time and again, drawn by its flowers, its scenery, its levada walks and its peace and tranquillity will doubtless hope that mass tourism will never arrive.

Geography

Madeira is volcanic in origin, the volcanic activity being underwater and pushing lava cones up from the sea bed. The cones broke surface during the Miocene Era of geological time, roughly 20 million years ago - at much the same time as the nearby Azores and Canary Islands formed. The volcanoes continued to pile up material, producing a sharp-sided island: just a short distance off-shore the sea depth is measured in hundreds of metres - about 80km (50 miles) to the west the depth has been measured to over 6,000m (20,000ft).

Successive volcanic eruptions deposited lava and ash, creating the diversity of rocks to be seen on the island, these ranging from hard basalt to the more easily eroded red-brown tufa. The winds and rains of ages have carved the softer rocks - sometimes sculpting strange shapes, which combine with the basalt to create the angular peaks of the highest mountains - sometimes creating undulating plateaux. The rain also created rivers, fast flowing rivers as Madeira is high in comparison to its size, which thrashed downhill, carving deep valleys, occasionally defined by steep cliffs.

The volcanic ash and weathered lava created a fertile soil in which windblown seeds took root. By the time man first arrived on Madeira the island was thickly clad with trees. Early farmers clearing the land by burning the forests, added wood ash to the soil making it even more fertile, a fertility which not only helped - and continues to help - the growth of sugar, vines, bananas and many other species of fruit and vegetables, but also the luxuriant growth of sub-tropical plant species for which Madeira is famous.

Food and Drink

Food

Madeiran cooking can be safely described as a mix of Portuguese and Arabic. As a relatively poor country Portugal tends towards food which is basic and hearty, rather than exotic, but on Madeira this simple cuisine is spiced in the Arabic tradition, most dishes using a mix of garlic, laurel, fennel, lemon and caraway seeds.

The menu reveals an immediate double contradiction. Since Madeira is an island you might expect fish to be a speciality. Yet Madeira's volcanic origins mean that there is no continental shelf,

Madeira

Festa do Vinho

Funchal

Terraces and Fruit Trees

The poios, terraces on the hillsides are one of Madeira's most remarkable features. The hillsides were not amenable to agriculture, not only because they were so steep, but because after the slopes had been stripped of their covering of trees, rain washed the fertile soil into the valleys - and much of it from there into the sea. To form the hillsides the Madeirans undid the damage caused by the rain, hauling wicker baskets of soil back up the slopes to create the terraces we see today. At first shored up by wooden poles, then by stone walls, the terraces are still maintained as they have been for centuries. They are too small, and too difficult of access, for machinery, so most work is carried out by hand, and the walls are too fragile (and too steep and high) for cattle to be allowed to wander freely.

The terraces climb the hillsides to about 700m (2,300ft) above which the climate is too harsh for crops. On the highest terraces vegetables are grown - cabbage and carrots, white and green beans, onions and potatoes. Lower down are the fruits - vines for wine, bananas for exports, and a wonderful variety of sub-tropical fruits to delight the palate. There are figs, prickly pears (sometimes known as cactus figs), passion fruit, papaya (also know as paw paw), mango and guava. Of the more exotic fruits the most unusual for the first time visitor is the custard apple (known locally as the anona, and sometimes known the sweet sop), a greyish-skinned fruit brought here from the Caribbean. It is a difficult fruit to eat and stay dry - be sure you have some moist wipes or access to a washroom for when you have finished, this is one of the world's juiciest fruits - and is often pressed to produce a refreshing drink. Another unusual fruit is the loquat, the Japanese medlar.

the sea plunging to vast depths just off-shore. No continental shelf means no easy fishing: in other parts of the world deep-sea fishing means few species caught infrequently. The double contradiction is that despite the lack of a continental shelf, fish are indeed to be found on the Madeiran menu, with a variety which apparently defies the idea that deep-sea fishing is hard work for limited returns. Deprived of the easy catches of their continental neighbours, Madeira's fishermen have perfected the use of very long lines to catch fish at great depth - up to 1,000m (3,300ft) deep. It is here that Madeira's greatest delicacy, the espada - named for the sword scabbard which the long thin fish resembles is caught. Espada - as anyone can discover by visiting the early morning fish markets - is an ugly, murderous looking fish. It is about 1m (3.25ft) long, and very thin shiny black with large eyes and rows of razor-sharp teeth. It lives at up to 800m (1/2 mile) deep, though is usually taken at around 500m (1,600ft). At those depths there is little light – hence the large eyes of this efficient predator. Unknown until the mid-nineteenth century, the espada is still a scientific mystery – where and when does it breed? does it lay eggs or give birth to live young? – but is landed by Madeira's night-fishermen by the several hundred tons annually.

But espada comes later in the menu. First there is a starter, though it has to be said that such culinary niceties are not highly regarded by the islanders, who have a limited number from which to choose. Sopa de tomate (sometimes called sopa de tomate e cebola, a far more accurate title) is a soup of chopped tomatoes and onions, sometimes with an added poached egg. A good alternative is caldo verde, a cabbage soup, usually a thin, clear soup, but occasionally thickened. Either of the soups will come with bread. Bolo de caco is a flat, light bread, made with maize flour, sometimes served with garlic butter. Pão de batata (or pão de casa) is a courser bread made from sweet potato flour. For something distinctly different, try lapas (limpets), usually served in garlic butter.

The main course could be espada. Traditionally the fish is served com banana, fried and topped with sliced banana, but is now more often served com vinto e alhos, that is marinated in wine and fried in olive oil. Other fish dishes include espadarte (swordfish), freira (like a cross between bream and mackerel), bodião (parrot fish) and several dozen more, including grouper, mullet, tuna (known as atum, though gaido, the bonito, is very similar: the difference is largely seasonal, bonito being caught in summer, tuna in autumn) and trout from the island's trout-farm. The fish could be served as paella (which might also include shellfish and prawns), caldeirada (the Madeiran equivalent of bouillabaisse), or cataplana, baked with herbs and served with rice. Apart from the rice dishes, fish is usually served with potatoes.

A rather more exotic fish dish is bacalhau, salted cod, which is grilled and served with potatoes and vegetables, or casseroled with onions, garlic and potatoes.

Meat is very expensive (in comparison to fish) as most has to be imported. However bife (beef), porco (pork), corço (lamb) and frango (chicken) are all available. These will usually be offered frito (roasted) or grelhedo (grilled). One speciality is espetada, a kebab of beef skewered on laurel (bay)

Ear Muffs or Ear Defenders?

The most often seen man's headgear is the barrete de lã, a knitted wool caps with ear flaps and an elaborate bobble.

It might be thought that the ear flaps were for use on cold days, but the Madeirans claim that the flaps are worn up during the day, and only lowered at night when a man goes home after a convivial evening with friends, the flaps keeping out the wife's questions about where he has been all this time......

sticks and cooked over an open fire, also of aromatic wood. Sadly many restaurants now serve espetada cooked on a grill, losing the gentle wood aromatics. Most meat dishes are served with French fries (chips) and vegetables or salad, though occasionally sweet potatoes or milho frito, deep-fried maize cubes are offered. The vegetables are likely to be white or green beans or chickpeas.

For dessert there will be ice cream of fruit salad. As the island's fruits include such exotics as passion fruit, prickly pear, figs, cherries, mangoes and the custard apple, each is likely to be excellent. There may be a small range of pudim (pudding), usually fruit blancmange or forms of mousse, and there may be cakes. Of the latter the speciality is bolo do mel, honey cake, a very heavy cake made with molasses. Bolo do mel keeps very well, and many visitors take it home as a souvenir or gift.

Drinks

Coffee is bica, served black in a small cup. Café grande is the same coffee, but more of it. If you want milk in your coffee ask for cappuccino or a chinesa (literally a Chinese lady) which is served in a large cup with a lot of milk.

Soft drinks are as elsewhere - Coca Cola and Pepsi Cola are heading for world domination - but there are also soft drinks made from exotic fruits.

Foreign beers are imported, but Coral is the island brewery, producing a light lager.

Wines are dealt with elsewhere in the book (see page 34-35). The local spirit is aguardente, a rum distilled from sugar cane. There are also some liqueurs: licor de castanha is made from chestnuts: it is gin-like and a speciality of Curral das Freiras. Maracujá is made from passion fruit and ginja from cherries. The pousada (guesthouse/resthouse) at Pico do Arieiro has a house speciality called poncha made from aguardente, honey and lemon juice. Walkers are recommended to try it after their hike!

Flora and Fauna

The destruction of Madeira's natural woodlands, together with the introduction of so many shrubs and trees from around the world, many of which have escaped the paths and gardens in which they were first grown, means it can be difficult to identify the indigenous island flora. It is most easily seen in the laurisilva, the laurel woods which, growing above the 700m (2,300ft) contour - which is the ceiling for crops on the terraced hillsides - survived the slash-and-burn clearances of the early settlers. There are said to be over 90 sub-species of laurel on the island, but the predominant trees are the Madeiran and Azorean (or Canary) laurels (Laurus indicus and Laurus azorica), the Til (Ocotea foetens), the Madeiran mahogany (the vinhático - Persea indico) and the ironwood (Appolonias barbujana). Higher up the mountains there is gorse and juniper and around 60 species of fern. Lower, but now very rarely seen, is the Dragon tree (Dracaena draco), which supplied a red dye called Dragon's Blood, the collection of which has almost made the tree extinct on the island.

The eucalyptus woods which are

Lavadas

Over 2m (77 inches) of rain falls annually on the northern part of Madeira, the prevailing wind forcing clouds on to the island's east-west running high ridge of mountains and the water they drop cascading down the northern slopes.

But the sun shines on the southern coast, making it the ideal place for agricultural - if it was not for the absence of rain. Sometimes it can be dry for the whole six months of summer.

It is said that the Moors solved the problems for the island's early settlers - probably Moorish slaves captured during one of the periodic battles for supremacy over the Iberian peninsula. In their North African homeland the Moors had become skilled at channelling water from places of abundance to places of shortage, and during the fifteenth, and throughout the sixteenth, century they created a series of channels to carry water from the highlands to the fields of the south. The channels were named levadas, the word deriving from the Portuguese levar, to carry. The engineering of the levadas is impressive. To make best use of the water the downhill gradient needed to be gentle, and to do this the channelling sometimes involved tunnelling through rock ridges and occasionally running the channels on the outside of rock faces, with huge drops beside them. Legend has it that some work on the channels was carried out by men working from wicker seats suspended by long ropes over these sheer drops. Numerous deaths occurred due to rope failure, or to men simply falling off the narrow walls of the channels.

The water in the levadas was utilised by the farmers whose land they crossed, each channel being fitted with a series of sluice gates which could be opened - on a strict rotation, for an allotted time - in turn. The first rush of levada construction served the island well, though new channels have occasionally been dug since. In recent times, assisted by grants from the European Union, several new channels have been constructed: unlike old open channels, these tend to use pipes, enclosing the water to reduce losses due to evaporation and to eliminate possible contamination.

now such a feature of the island as a result from a planned programme of re-afforestation, the trees being brought from Australia.

Of the flowers, many of the species seen are escapes, but there are still indigenous varieties - Madeiran geranium, yellow foxglove on the lower slopes and Madeiran violet and Madeira saxifrage on the mountains. It is estimated that

The open levadas needed to be walked more or less constantly to ensure that they had not become blocked or partially blocked, to ensure that sluice gates worked efficiently, and to make sure that no one was illicitly jamming their sluices slightly open so as to increase their share of the water. To help these levada checkers, paths were built beside the channels and these paths can be used by visitors to explore the island. There are a couple of thousand kilometres of levadas, though not all of the system can be (or is worth) exploring. The best levadas explore the scenic highlights of the island, cutting through the finest scenery from their starts high in the mountains. Some of the paths have sections which are extremely exposed and, as they have no guard-rails, they are usable only by the sure-footed walker who is not bothered by exposure to huge drops. But in the main the paths beside the channels offer a safe way of exploring the best of Madeiran scenery.

there are 30 species of plants and flower which are indigenous to the island, many of them growing in the highlands where the escaped plants fare less well. The large daisies, which grow in several colours and can be seen on the roadsides of the highland roads, are particularly lovely. Of the garden species the most eye-catching are, of course, the orchids, hundreds of varieties, many

Festivals & Events

Only the festivals at the largest towns and villages are given here. The Tourist Information Office can supply details of festivals at smaller villages.

January

5th
Festival of Sao Amaro at Santa Cruz
20th
Festival of Sao Sebastião at Câmara de Lobos

February

Carnival season, with events resembling the famous Rio carnival held all over the island. There are usually processions on Shrove Tuesday, with the carnival events taking place on the Saturday before and lasting until Tuesday itself.

Festa do Campadres at Santana.

April

Flower festivals are held all over the island. The most famous, and the most flamboyant, is that in Funchal towards the end of the month. The highlight is the parade of flower-decked floats.

May/June

The Madeiran Music Festival begins in late May and lasts for several weeks.

June

29th
Festival of São Pedro, the patron saint of fisherman, with a procession of boats at Ribiera Brava and Câmara de Lobos.
Also a service at Capela de São Pedro, Porto Santo.

July

17th
Festival of Nossa Senhora at Arco de Calheta.
22nd
Festivals of Santa Maria Madalena at Madalena do Mar and Porto Moniz.
31st
Festival of Santissimo Sacramento at Caniço. This includes the lighting of fires on the hillside above the village.

August

15th
Festival of the Assumption. This

---

with only a Latin name, being grown and offered for sale. Orchids travel well, especially if packed by the better flower shops - they will pack into a cardboard box which is best carried in the hold of your plane where it is less likely to be crushed - lasting several weeks when you get home. Of the other plants, bougainvillaea will be seen by all visitors, as will the spectacular Bird of Paradise flower, both growing just about everywhere. There are also wonderful varieties of lily and iris, and it the drier areas splendid cacti.

is held at villages throughout the islands, but the major festival, lasting three days, is at Monte.

August also sees the Madeiran Wine Rally which counts towards the Europe Cup.

September

1st Sunday

Festival of Bom Jesus at Ponta Delgada.

8th-9th

Festival of Senhora dos Milagres in Machico, including a night-time procession.

3rd Sunday

Festival of Nossa Senhora da Piedade at Caniçal including a procession of boats.

September is the time of the grape harvest and there are numerous grape/wine festivals throughout the island. The major events are at Funchal and Estreito de Câmara Lobos. At the latter visitors can join in with the traditional grape pressing, taking off their shoes and rolling up their trousers (unless they are in skirts of course) to tread with the locals. Most of the festivals - and that at Estreito de Câmara de Lobos is no exception - involve music, dancing, eating and the consumption of a lot of wine.

September also sees the apple fair at Ponta do Pargo.

October

1st Sunday

Festival of Nossa Senhora de Rosario at São Vicente.

November

1st

Chestnut Festival at Curral das Freiras

December

8th

Lights are put up in all towns and villages. Funchal, especially takes on a magical appearance.
The lights stay up until 6th January

31st

Fireworks display in many places, but most famously in Funchal

---

Of animal life, the only indigenous mammal is a species of bat, though there are animals introduced by man – rabbits and feral domestic animals. There are several species of frog and a single species of lizard. The Desertas Islands is home to a fearsome poisonous spider and is one of the last strongholds of the monk seal.

Only when birds are considered does the island excel, with over 200 recorded species. Madeira has its own sub-species of the robin, chaffinch and firecrest, has wild canaries and is famous

Market, Funchal

Riding on the Monte toboggan

Levada

Welcome to Madeira

Coralina Cristada

Massaroco

27

for the spectacled warbler. The warbler is a small, somewhat insignificant bird. That could not be said of the hoopoe, another island resident, a spectacular bird of salmon pink, black and white with a bold crest. Most visitors will see some seabirds too, but the real enthusiast will need to travel towards the Desertas Islands for a glimpse of the island's rarities.

Madeiran Costume

The traditional folk dress of the islanders is today rarely seen, even at Festivals, though the women flower sellers of Funchal still wear it. Worn by women and young girls alike, it consists of a knee-length woollen skirt in stripes of red alternating with stripes of yellow, green, blue, white or black, the actual pattern being defined by the village of birth - somewhat like the Scottish tartan. The skirt is worn with a white blouse and an embroidered red waistcoat. Across one shoulder is a scarf, also red and edged with another colour.

Men wear white shirts and baggy, white, knee-length trousers, sometimes with a waist sash of red and coloured stripes, the pattern again differing from village to village. This traditional costume is worn by the basket sled men of Monte, though they wear conventional length trousers, usually with a belt, but occasionally with a white cummerbund. The sled men also wear straw 'boaters' with a black band, which is not part of the traditional dress. That, for both sexes, is the carapuça, a black or blue skull cap with a long tassel (actually more a spike than a tassel as it is semi-rigid). Anciently, the length of the tassel was an indication of the wearer's social status.

On their feet both sexes wear botas, an ankle-length boot of cow or goat leather turned over at the top. The boots - which are also called botacha - are usually trimmed with a red band.

Music and Dance

Most visitors to Madeira will see a performance of fado, a form of song believed to be Moorish in origin. Fado means 'fate', and songs can be as mournful as the name. Their overt sadness, a lamentation for things past, unnerved Salazar who banned it in case the Portuguese yearning for a better world resulted in his overthrow. But though popular on Madeira, fado is an introduced, mainland, song. More traditional is desafio (sometimes called despique), a curious song in which a group (usually just two) of singers report on recent events in their village. More exuberant is the charamba, a song for two or more singers who take turns to insult each other.

Both local forms of song are accompanied by the guitar, or a band using traditional instruments. The braguinha is a small, four-stringed instrument, somewhat like a ukulele. The rajão is a larger, five-stringed instrument. There is usually a violin (rabeca) or the viola de arme, an eight-stringed violin, and a piano accordion. Two very curious instruments are the reque-reque, a form of rattle, and the brinquinho in which rings of wooden dolls slide up and down a wooden stick. The dolls have bells and castonholas (a form of castanets) and provide a percussive accompaniment to the music when the dolls are moved.

Until the early twentieth century there was a folk dancing tradition on Madeira, with the numerous small farming settlements having there own forms of dance. Then the tradition began to die. Today its decline has been arrested by local groups who have revived the old dances, and these may be seen at festivals and exhibitions, though rarely in the spontaneous local events as they once were. The island's most famous dance is the bailinho, a form which is usually accompanied by singing as well as music.

Festivals

To many who have visited Madeira at different times of year it might seem that the islands have a festival - at one place or another - on every day. This is not true of course, but with each village having its own festival at some time during the year there are certainly a large number. A village festival usually starts with a ramario, a pilgrimage procession to the church, but rapidly transforms into an arraial when a good time is had by all, with singing and dancing, local bands of musicians, the eating of espetadas and the drinking of a great deal of wine. The festival usually starts with a fireworks display: historians believing that in the days of poor communications this was the best way of letting neighbouring villages know about the festival and inviting them to attend.

Some of the ramarios began as a promessa, a vow, usually made by medieval villagers in thanks to the village's patron saint for deliverance from pirates, plague or fire. Of these the greatest is that on Assumption Day at Monte, a festival to which pilgrims from all over the island make their way.

1. Funchal

Opposite: Funchal
Left: Doca swimming pools do Cavacas Fuchal

Madeira's capital is an elegant town, and will be even more so when the new 'expressway' under construction to the north of the town has removed some (hopefully most) of the traffic which currently clogs its streets and overburden the air with noise and fumes.

Just less than half of Madeira's population live in Funchal, their houses filling the space between the gently curved shore of its bay and the dramatic peaks which back it. The peaks rise quickly to over 1,000m (3,300ft), the northern part of the town climbing steep slopes, the houses linked by equally steep streets whose ascent raises a sweat even when taken casually.

The city is named for the sweet-smelling fennel (funcho in Portuguese) which the first explorers found growing in profusion on the banks of the three rivers that empty into the bay. Those first explorers were the men of João Gonçalves Zarco, one of the discoverers of Madeira. After finding Porto Santo in 1418 Zarco returned in 1419, sailing on to discover Madeira in 1420. Zarco's first base was Câmara de Lobos, from where he soon found the bay, and the

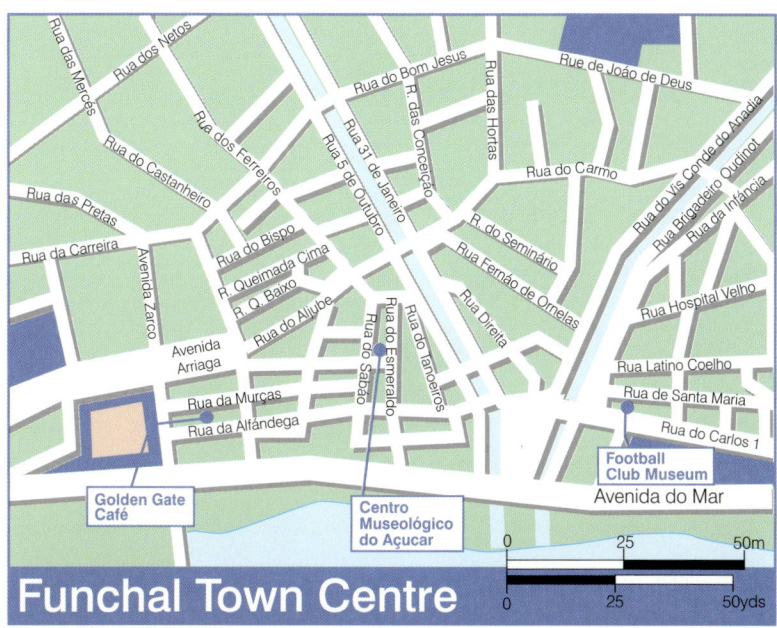

Funchal Town Centre

31

Madeira

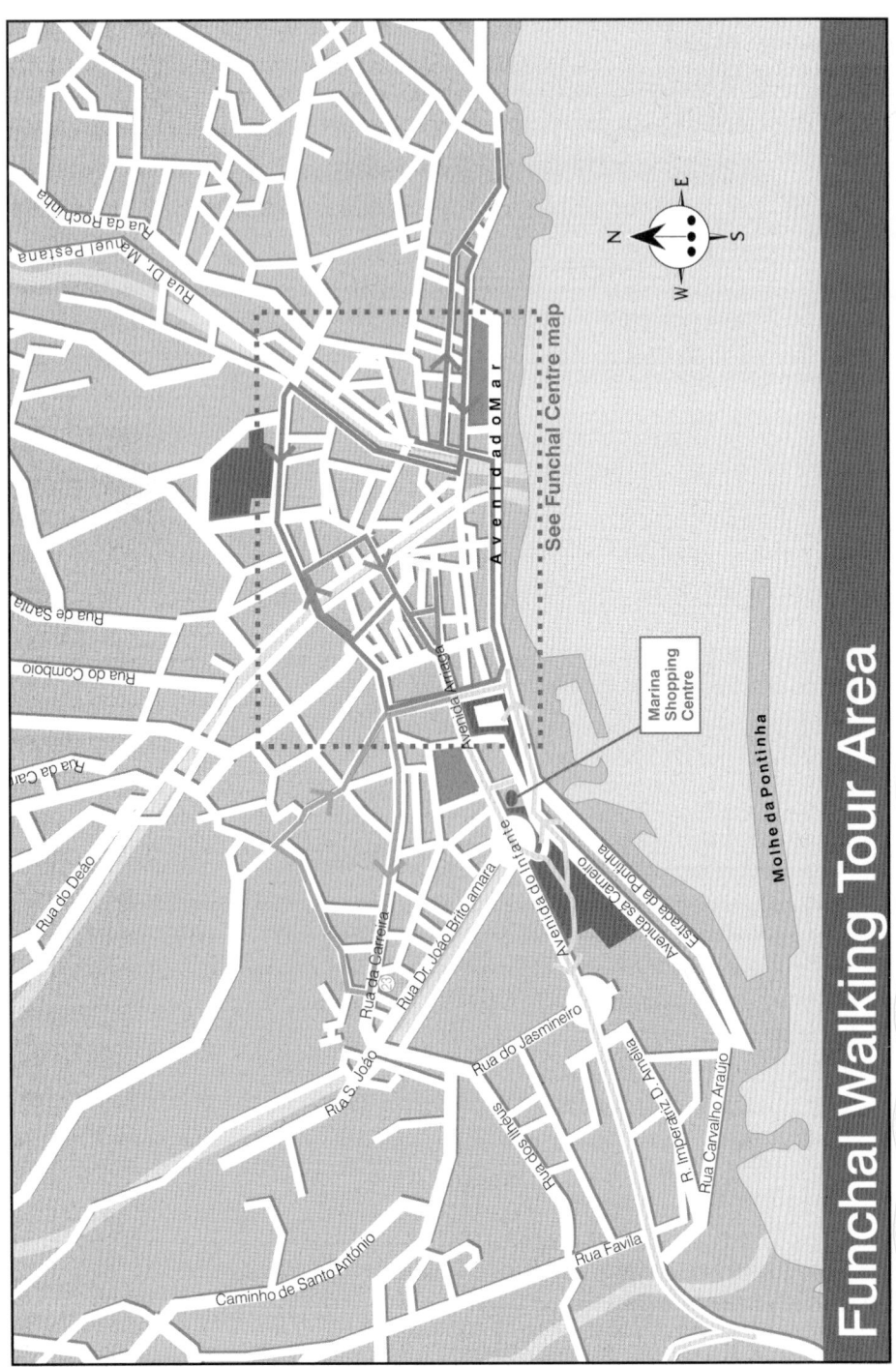

rivers which now lie within the town limits. It is ironical, given the basis for Funchal's name, that the first thing Zarco did was to strip the river banks. One legend has it that a bush fire, started after tree felling for building or ship repair, got out of control and destroyed the vegetation. Within five years Funchal had become the island's capital, Zarco moving here from Câmara.

At first Funchal consisted of a few farm settlements and Zarco's mansion and offices, but the rise of the sugar trade rapidly increased the town's population. In about 1452 the first slaves were shipped to Madeira (from Africa and the Canary Islands) and the valleys of Funchal's rivers - the most fertile land before the first of the *levadas*, the Madeiran water channels, had been constructed - were soon filled with waving cane. It is said that in 1478 Christopher Columbus sailed into Funchal's bay on a mission to buy sugar. If he really did visit (as we shall see, at Porto Santo, not everyone is convinced of Madeira's connection to the great explorer), Columbus was not alone, the cane fields making Funchal a prosperous place. It was occasionally called 'Little Lisbon' for the richness and elegance of its houses and churches: in 1514 it was created a see, becoming Portugal's third biggest city, after Lisbon and Porto, with a population of over 5,000.

But Funchal's wealth attracted not only entrepreneurs and traders, but pirates, the city being the target of frequent attacks. A fortress and town wall were required, but the decision to build them came at the wrong time. The yield of Madeira's cane fields was falling, years of intensive production exhausting the once-rich volcanic soil. Competition from Portugal's Brazilian colonies was also reducing Funchal's prosperity. The town walls took years to build and when they were finally completed (in 1542) they were really adequate only against minor raids. When, in 1566, the Frenchman Bertrand de Montluc arrived with a fleet of ships and a large band of well-armed men, the walls were rapidly stormed and Funchal's defences over-run. The city's fortress (the Fortress of São Lourenço) seemed formidable enough, but though it had cannons, Funchal's finances did not run to either cannonballs or gunpowder and the French took it easily, slaughtering not only the soldiers who manned it, but the townsfolk who had fled to it for safety.

Having destroyed Funchal's limited attempted to defend itself and killed many of its inhabitants, De Montluc's men then systematically pillaged the mansions of the city's rich merchants, stealing everything they could move. They also looted the churches (though they virtually ignored the cathedral: whether this was by accident or design has never been truly established - an old Madeiran legend claims that the clergy placed the greatest treasures in the coffin of an official who had, just days before, been buried in the chancel, reasoning, correctly, that the French would not open the tombs).

After De Montluc's raid the fortress was re-armed and the town wall improved, and Funchal rapidly regained its former prosperity. Indeed, after wine production had replaced sugar as Madeira's main 'industry', the city became

French entrants for a cross-Atlantic race assemble in Funchal Marina

phylloxera, a vicious vine disease, was brought to Madeira from America (American vines being mildew-resistant), an accident which virtually destroyed the wine industry. Phylloxera-resistant vines were planted, but the industry never regained its former glories, many of the wine merchants selling up and leaving. Bananas and tourism saved Madeira. In Funchal the former did not lead to prosperity rivalling the wine trade, a fact reflected in the newer buildings which indicate a cautious, somewhat pessimistic view of local economics, rather than the regal optimism of the earlier times. Tourism produced the hotels that now dominate the west end of Funchal's bay.

From those hotels it is a 30 minute walk to the heart of the city, but if you plan to explore on foot (the best way as Funchal has a host of curious corners) it might be better to take a taxi: the steep

even more prosperous. Many of the wine merchants who came to Funchal were English. At first they came to avoid a ban on the export of all European (meaning non-British) goods to the American colonies. Madeira was not covered by the ban and so the merchants could export its wines without incurring the wrath of parliament. Later, (in the early eighteenth century), when England and Portugal became allies, the English gained a near monopoly on the export of Madeiran wine. These rich English merchants were responsible for many of the great mansions that give the city its rich, elegant feel, and also for some of the gardens for which Madeira is now famous.

In 1852 mildew killed 90% of the island's vines. The regrowth of the wine trade was slow and then, in the 1870s,

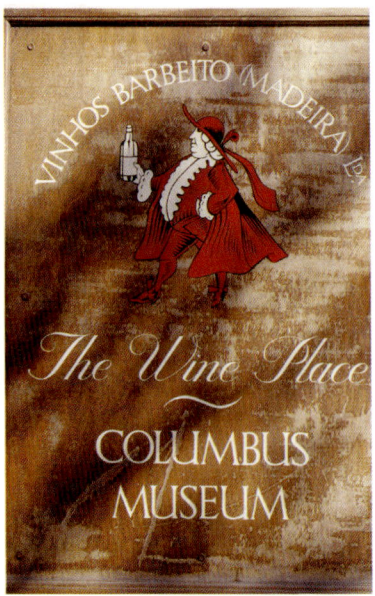

Sign for the Columbus Museum at the Diogos Wine shop in Avenida Arriaga

Funchal

(sometimes stepped) cobbled streets of the old town offer enough exercise.

Exploring the City

There is so much of interest to see in Funchal that despite the main sights all lying within 1km (a little over 1/2mile) of the cathedral, it is an epic walk to visit them all in one go. Here, a number of shorter tours - which can be mixed and matched at will - is suggested.

Completing them all allows the visitor to claim to have seen the best Funchal has to offer.

Walking Tour 1

Heading west from Zarco

At the centre of the intersection of Avenida Arriaga and Avenida Zarco

35

Madeira

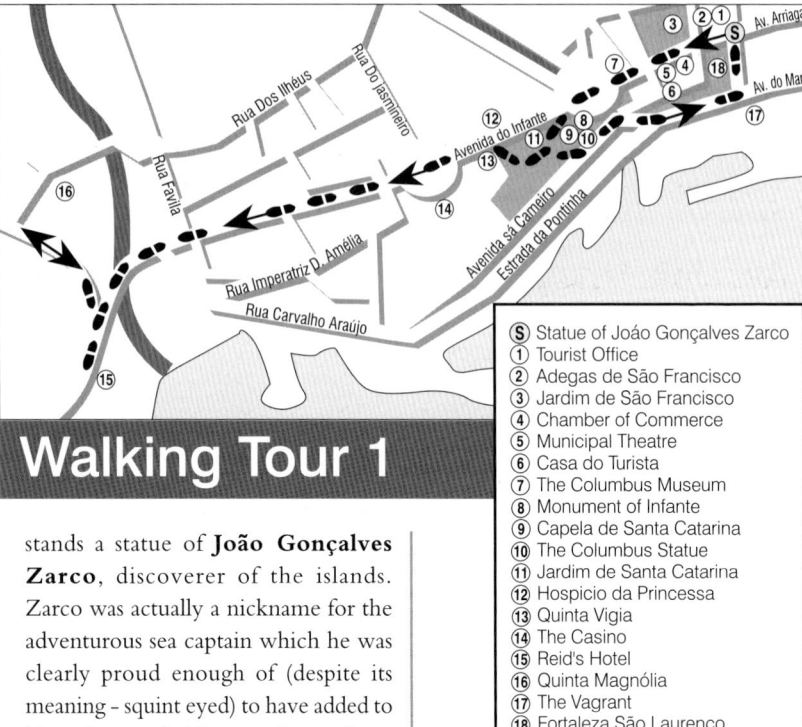

- Ⓢ Statue of Joáo Gonçalves Zarco
- ① Tourist Office
- ② Adegas de São Francisco
- ③ Jardim de São Francisco
- ④ Chamber of Commerce
- ⑤ Municipal Theatre
- ⑥ Casa do Turista
- ⑦ The Columbus Museum
- ⑧ Monument of Infante
- ⑨ Capela de Santa Catarina
- ⑩ The Columbus Statue
- ⑪ Jardim de Santa Catarina
- ⑫ Hospicio da Princessa
- ⑬ Quinta Vigia
- ⑭ The Casino
- ⑮ Reid's Hotel
- ⑯ Quinta Magnólia
- ⑰ The Vagrant
- ⑱ Fortaleza São Lourenço

Walking Tour 1

stands a statue of **Joáo Gonçalves Zarco**, discoverer of the islands. Zarco was actually a nickname for the adventurous sea captain which he was clearly proud enough of (despite its meaning - squint eyed) to have added to his real name. In his stone-frozen form, Zarco gazes, with squint-free attention, towards the sea. The statue was the work of the Madeiran sculptor Francisco Franco (more of whose work can be seen at the museum in his honour) and was erected in 1934. Over Zarco's left shoulder in the baroque building housing the government of the autonomous region of Madeira, a splendid building with fine ironwork, excellent azulejos in the vast entranceway and a neat courtyard with a playful fountain.

Diagonally opposite the government offices is the **Fortaleza São Lourenço**. The fortress was built in 1513, during the reign of King Manuel I, though only the south-eastern tower (which bears the king's arms) remains from that period. The original fortress consisted of more than that tower, but not much more, a fact which, combined with the lack of gunpowder and cannonballs, allowed the French pirates to over-run it with such ease. Today the cannons that poke above the red-flowered poinsettia trees (from the battlements on the seaward side) are as ornamental as they were when De Montluc arrived. The fortress walls themselves were largely ornamental when they were built: work continued on the fortress until the nineteenth century by which time the threats to Funchal had all but vanished. By the time work was completed the fortress had become the palace of the island's governor and the military commander. It remains so, explaining the occasional name of Palácio de Sao Lourenço. A statue of St Lawrence himself stands above the main entrance: the ship that brought Zarco to Madeira was named for the saint. The entrance, in Avenida Zarco, a street notable for its yellow-blossomed tipuana trees, is guarded by sword-carrying soldiers. Visitors are not allowed into the fortress on a general basis, but groups can apply for permission.

Avenida Arriaga

Now head westwards along Avenida Arriaga (with the fortress on your left). The pedestrian section of the street is a delight, a mosaic of pale limestone and dark basalt, the latter in elegant curved, almost floral, shapes. The mosaic dates from the nineteenth century (when such pavements were a Portuguese fashion) and is one of the best preserved on the island. The shading trees are jacaranda, which are heavy with pale lilac blossom from April until early June.

Soon, Funchal's Tourist Office is passed on the right. Just beyond is the **Adegas de São Francisco**, a section of an old Franciscan monastery now occupied by the Madeira Wine Company. The monastery was built in the sixteenth century, but closed in 1834 when all monastic orders in Portugal were dissolved. With its wooden balconies, hung with wisteria in true romantic fashion, around an old cobbled courtyard, the building is worth the visit in its own right. The Madeira Wine Company is a partnership of some of the oldest, best-established names in the wine trade, and accounts for about 30% of the island's exports. Within the *adegas* (literally a 'lodge') there are almost 500,000 litres of wine, stored in vast barrels, so big that the floors have needed reinforcing with beams which are equally vast. It is said that many of these beams were obtained from ships wrecked on the Madeiran coast.

Within the lodge visitors can join a guided tour (lasting about an hour) that includes an audio-visual presentation on the history of Madeira wine; a visit to the lodge's own coopering (barrel-making) shop where chestnut, mahogany and American oak are turned into barrels, and existing barrels are repaired and re-hooped; and a look at the various stages in Madeira preparation. There is also a museum of the Company and the trade, the former including leather-bound ledgers, the latter an impressively huge grape press. The tour also includes a testing of the finished product and the chance to buy a bottle (or several). The shop includes bottles of rare vintage, so expensive carrying it would make you nervous.

Just beyond the Wine Lodge is the **Jardim de São Francisco** where the remaining buildings of the Franciscan monastery once stood. Little is left of the monastery, though the carved stone coat-of-arms which once graced the entranceway remains. The statue of St Francis was erected in 1982. The site was turned into a small public garden in 1878 and with its shady trees and a cool fountain/pool is a marvellous place, enjoyed by young and old. The trees are a mix of palms and some more unusual tropical varieties - frangipani, magnolia, tulip trees, red sandalwood and silk-cotton. Here, as in most places in the city, many of the trees are labelled. Right beside the pavement, ducks swim on a little pool into which two stone boys persuade themselves to jump.

Beside the park the little church is for

Madeira Wine

Although production did not start in earnest until after the decline of the sugar industry, Madeiran wine was already famous in late sixteenth century England, Shakespeare mentioning it in several plays. Its ability to create glowing roses is mentioned in Henry IV and, famously, in Richard III, the Duke of Clarence ends in a butt of malmsey (though he been stabbed several times before). Shakespeare's chronology can be questioned - Madeira had not been discovered at the time the action in the plays took place - but his knowledge of Madeira wine cannot.

The first Madeiran vineyards were planted with Cretan grapes (called malvasia, a corruption of Monemvasia, the Greek port from which they were shipped). The island's volcanic soil and these grapes produced an acidic, but sweet wine. The wine was popular with wine drinkers in Europe, but was also popular with ships' captain. Barrels of wine made good ballast for their ships, as well being good for trade, and it was also a cheap drink for the sailors. (Madeiran wine, being very fruity also had a lot of Vitamin C, the scurvy preventative and so kept the crew healthy, though whether this was fully understood or just a happy by-product is debatable). The story is told that after one voyage to the East a ship returned to Madeira where, to his annoyance, the captain found a full barrel of wine left in the hold. Told to pour the wine overboard the crew decided to dispose of it in the more traditional way. To their amazement the wine was delicious, the best they had ever tested. Unsure of what had happened, the wine merchants persuaded other captains to carry barrels to and from the East. The same thing happened again, and soon whole ship loads of wine were being carried backwards and forwards, and sold as Vinho de Roda (round-trip wine).

Back on Madeira experiments were carried out to see if the shipboard conditions could be replicated. What was the cause of the dramatic improvement in the wine's quality - was it the equatorial heat? was it the rolling of the ship? It is claimed that an abbot was the first to succeed in reproducing the 'new' taste, warming wine in an estufa (greenhouse) and gently agitating it. Soon all Madeira wine was being processed in similar fashion.

Then, during the Napoleonic Wars, Napoleon's occupation of Iberia allowed his forces to blockade Madeira, ending the English trade in the wine. On the islands vats of unsold wine accumulated and, in despair at its loss due to souring, the merchants added brandy to the wine, hoping to prevent further fermentation. To their amazement they created a fortified wine which was not only better than standard Madeira but which lasted indefinitely. A famous story tells of the ship taking Napoleon to exile in St Helena calling at Madeira and taking on a pipe (418 litres) of wine to ease the Emperor's loneliness. In fact Napoleon did not drink the wine and after his death it was, in 1840, returned to the island, transferred to demijohns and sold as 'Napoleon Madeira'. A demijohn was opened when Sir Winston Churchill visited the island in 1950. The great man is said to have been thrilled at the prospect of drinking a wine grown when Marie Antoinette was still alive: and the wine was still excellent. As an interesting aside, it is said that more gallons of 'Napoleon Madeira' have now been sold than could ever have been grown in a single summer!

The earliest Madeira was made by the traditional foot trampling method, but the grapes are now pressed mechanically. (Here, as elsewhere, the real wine connoisseur regrets the new method: feet were gentler, not crushing either stems or pips which add a bitter taste to the juice). The juice is then placed in huge vats (concrete for the cheaper wines, wood for the better quality) and fermented. Spirit is added at this time, taking the strength to about 17%. The wine is then given the equatorial treatment, being heated gently to about 50°C and then cooled, the full process taking 2-12 months. The difference in time depends on the method of heating. The shorter times use large tanks, heating coils and circulation pumps. Better wines are produced in a process taking 4-6 months with the wine stored in lodges (never underground) where gentle heat and the warmth of the sun do the job. The very best wines still use vats beneath glass. In all cases the wine is open to the air. The chemistry of the process is not understood (despite scientific analysis) but it is known that heating any other wine - and definitely if it is open to the air - destroys it. Only Madeira wines can (and must) be so abused.

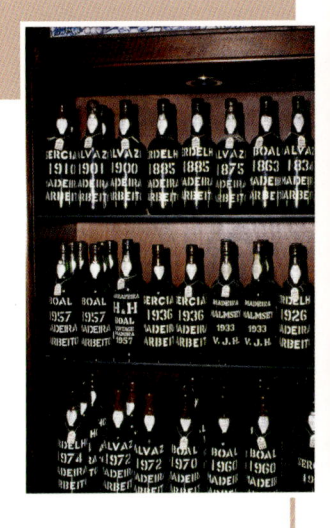

The final part of the process is a maturation in wooden casks. Again this is with the wine open to the air. Evaporation losses - the maturation can take decades for the best wines - mean that the vats are topped up regularly. The added wine must be of a specific type: for 'vintage' it must be from the same year and grape type, for 'special' it must be the same grape type, but not necessarily the same year; for soleras, the more usual form, the wine is blended.

The wine that finally emerges is one of four types. Malmsey (still occasionally called malvasia) is the best known: it is a dark brown wine, the sweetest of all and drunk after meals. Bual (or Boal in Portuguese) is lighter and less sweet, and is a recommended dessert wine. Verdelho is medium dry: it is a beautiful golden colour and can be both an aperitif and a dessert wine. Sercial is from a particular type of grape which thrives on higher slopes: it is a dry wine, usually drunk as an aperitif.

Madeira's tiny Presbyterian community, built in 1861 to the pattern of the home-town kirks of Scottish traders. The exploits of one particular Scottish Calvinist, Dr Robert Kalley almost led to a diplomatic incident. Kalley was accused of trying to convert the islanders to Calvinism as part of a British

Azulejos

Despite the fact that azul is Portuguese for blue, and azulejos tiles are invariably blue and white, the name does not derive from the word. It actually derives from the Arabic word zuleyche meaning 'small polished stone'. The Persians invented the use of small stone mosaics as an adornment for buildings, the Arabs borrowing the idea and eventually exporting it to Spain when that country came under Moorish rule. The mosaics developed from polished stone to relief tiles, the pattern being die-stamped on to a clay tablet. The tiles were coloured, with oil added to grooves in the tile (or, occasionally, oiled string being laid across the tile) to prevent the colours from mixing.

The Koran forbids the representation of animals and humans in art, so whereas the Persian mosaics had been lively with plants and animals, the Arabic tiles had geometric patterns - but intricate patterns of great beauty, a form now know as Arabesque. In Spain tile production remained with the Moorish communities even after the country became Christian. At first the Moors who remained in Spain were allowed to maintain their Islamic faith and customs if they took an oath of loyalty to a Christian noble or the king. Such people were called Mujédares. The tile - and other - work they produced, still based on geometric patterns, has become known as Mujedar. The finest example of the form can be seen on the spire of Funchal's cathedral.

The spire also incorporates an advance in tile production which evolved in Renaissance Italy. There, flat-surfaced tiles were covered in a white glaze on to which the decoration was painted before final glazing, a style known as majolica. The new form was taken up enthusiastically in Portugal. To stop the colours running before glazing the tiles had to be small, but large pictures could be created by using many tiles, a system known as azulejos de tapete - literally carpet tiles. In Iberia the tiles were not only used as decoration, but as a form of damp-proofing and insulation, with whole walls (both internal and external) being covered. At about the same time, Portuguese traders returning from China brought examples of Chinese porcelain with its patterns composed entirely of blue and white. This style was taken up and soon the rich colours of early tiles were replaced by pictures only in white and shades of blue. It is that style which has been maintained. All over the island visitors will see examples of azulejos with pictures from the island's history or religious scenes created from the square tiles.

plot to annex Madeira. In 1846 a new Portuguese governor further accused the British of transporting Madeirans to mainland Portugal (a statement of truth though the motives were denied). The governor, assisted by a Funchal Jesuit, incited the locals to riot against Madeiran Calvinists. Dr Kalley was lucky to escape with his life (he went to Brazil, opened a church and applied his missionary zeal to both Portuguese and native Brazilians) and many Calvinists were badly beaten. The movement went underground for many years, but is now accepted.

Opposite the park is the Madeira **Chamber of Commerce**, housed in a building that once housed the Café Ritz, explaining the *azulejos* showing scenes from late nineteenth century socialite living - folk in hammocks being transported uphill, local crafts (embroidery and wickerwork) and general island scenes: the old funicular to Monte etc. The inside of the building has beautiful stuccoed ceilings, chandeliers and stairways, but is very rarely open to the public, though you could pretend to be interested in a Toyota, as part of the building is now a car showroom. Next door is the **Municipal Theatre**, built in 1885 and named for Baltazar Diaz, a local playwright. It was built in deluxe style, with four tiers of boxes, exquisite carvings and painted ceilings, but is rarely used for productions anywhere near as great as the decoration. If there is a film on, or just an exhibition it is worth a visit to admire the tasteful opulence. The Café do Teatro, on the town end of the theatre, is a good place for a coffee.

Turn left just beyond the theatre to reach the **Casa do Turista** - the 'Famous Shop' as it terms itself - a shop selling Madeiran and Portuguese crafts which, with its elegant furnishings and stock, is almost a museum of crafts. Back on Avenida Arriaga it is now a short step to the Rotunda do Infante, a roundabout named for the Infante (Prince) Henry the Navigator. Prince Henry. On the roundabout - to the right - is the Diogos Wine Shop, one of the best place in the city to buy wine - some of their wines are over 200 years old and cost hundreds of pounds. The shop's basement also houses an excellent Columbus Museum, with a record of his life, charts of the period, model ships and other period memorabilia.

Henry the Navigator

Prince Henry, 1394-1460, the son of King João I, was a collector of all things to do with the world beyond Portugal. Maps, navigational aids, accounts of voyages were all brought to a centre at Sagres on the Algarve where the Prince evaluated it. By a combination of bribery, orders and threats the Prince persuaded his captains to sail to Africa and beyond. Prince Henry is credited with the design of the caravel which, if true, is ironical as it is believed that he made only one sea journey in his lifetime. A fine bronze statue of the Prince gazes out across the roundabout which bears his name. It is fitting that his view includes a globe (held by 'sea' horses) in the fountain at the roundabout's centre, a tribute to the role of the Prince and Portuguese sailors in exploring the unknown world beyond Europe.

Funchal at night

Above: The Cloisters of the Convent of Santa Clara

Right: A flower-draped house near the British Cemetery

42

Jardim de Santa Catarina

Cross the Rotunda. Ahead is Avenida do Infante, but go past Prince Henry to reach the Jardim de Santa Catarina, another beautiful public park. The park was laid out in 1948, utilising what had been a cemetery. Here, too, there are numerous exotic trees and shrubs. There is also a pleasant lake with black swans, several aviaries, some old relics of the sugar industry, an adventure playground for children and a fine open-air cafe. Above the lake is a bronze statue by Francisco Franco representing the *Semeador*, the sower, a representation of Madeira's rural past.

At the Rotonda end of the park is another bronze statue (of Cristovâo Colombo - Christopher Columbus) stands near the **Capela de Santa Catarina**. It is claimed that the chapel stands on the site of the first to have been erected on the island (in 1425), by Constança Rodrigues, the wife of João Gonçalves Zarco. That first chapel was of wood: the present stone chapel dates from the seventeenth century (though it has been modified several times), but some experts believe the little bell tower dates from an earlier stone building. The holy water stoup beneath the entrance canopy is also earlier than the present chapel, the floral carvings dating it to the early sixteenth century. Sadly the little chapel is now always locked, and is in need of attention.

Regain Avenida do Infante from close to the lake, and continue uphill to see the **Quinta Vigia**. A *quinta* is a mansion (sometimes the estate around a mansion) Quinta Vigia being one of several mansions that occupied this favoured site overlooking the harbour, all of them built in the late eighteenth/early nineteenth century. Quinta Vigia is usually associated with Elizabeth of Austro-Hungary, the young and beautiful wife of Emperor Franz Josef I.

It is usually said that the Empress (affectionately known as Sisi by her husband) came here to overcome tuberculosis, but it seems more likely to have been to escape the excruciating boredom of the royal court in Vienna and the continuous belligerent interference of her mother-in-law. Sisi came on the British royal yacht *Victoria and Albert* (loaned by a thoughtful Queen Victoria) and though the climate improved her health, Madeira turned out to be even more boring than Vienna. '*If I had known what it was like I would have gone elsewhere*' she wrote to a friend, going on to note that the air was invigorating, but there was surely more to life than breathing. She found Funchal dirty, the steep, cobbled streets a trial which made a pleasant stroll purgatory, and eventually refused to leave the mansion, spending her time playing cards and weeping with boredom. Despite Sisi's view of the capital, Madeira still proudly remembers her visit. Even more astonishingly, she came again some 30 years later, staying in Reid's Hotel.

But the place where Sisi's visit is remembered is a fraud, Quinta Vigia is not the real mansion. That stood where the casino and hotel complex now stand, having been bulldozed to make way for the new buildings. To purge the guilt of that act of vandalism, the island government renamed the only surviving mansion Quinta Vigia and use it to entertain (and as a residence for) important visitors. Quinta Vigia was originally Quinta Lambert and is associated with two even gloomier episodes in Madeiran history. It was here that the Brazilian Empress Amelia (widow of Portugal's King Pedro IV) brought her daughter, Princess Marie Amelia, who really did have tuberculosis. The Empress loved Madeira and the islanders returned here love, but neither their enthusiasm for the visit, nor the sea air could help the Princess, who died here at the age of just 22. It is said that virtually the whole island turned out to watch here coffin being taken on board a ship for transport back to Brazil.

After the Empress had escorted here daughter's coffin from the mansion it lay empty for years, but was then bought by the Russian Comte de Lambert. It is said that the Comte had become involved in a love triangle with a Russian general and a lady, and that the men had agreed to settle the issue in the traditional way: they would draw lots, the loser committing suicide. Though arguably more sanitised than a duel (in which both men might be killed or injured, or neither killed, which would have been seen as worse) this procedure seems utterly appalling. Nevertheless the two agreed and the lots were drawn. The general lost and dutifully killed himself. But far from being the winner, Lambert was distraught. Turning his back on Russia he retired to this Madeiran mansion. Here he would spend days staring out to sea. The Comte was accompanied by his wife (was she having an affair with the general, or was the lady of the triangle someone else?) and when he eventually died she sold the mansion and left the island. Quinta Lambert, as it was then called, became sadly neglected, but after the demolition of the real Quinta Vigia it was refurbished and renamed. It is occasionally possible to visit the mansion, but even then only the gardens and private chapel are open. The entrance is in Avenida do Infante.

The **Casino** and hotel that replaced

Sisi - the Fairy-Tale Empress

When the boredom and troubles at the Habsburg court finally became too much for Empress Elizabeth she left her husband and fought for, and won, a custody battle for her children in a revolutionary decision which endeared her to her people. She also rewrote the ending of Shakespeare's A Midsummer's Night's Dream placing the donkey's head on the Duke - a gesture which everyone realised was an insult to her estranged husband. Sisi refused to allow herself to be photographed after she reached 35 so that she would always be remembered as youthfully beautiful, and was murdered by an Italian anarchist in Geneva - the tragic, romantic death which heroines require. Sisi is now a cult figure in Austria and becoming one in Madeira. In Austria they are even making Barbie dolls in her likeness - perhaps in a year or two they will be Madeiran souvenirs.

the old mansions were designed by the Brazilian architect Oscar Niemeyer (who also designed Brasilia). It is a near replica of the lower section of his cathedral in Brasilia, a design he said was inspired by the Crown of Thorns, seemingly a curiously inappropriate idea for a casino. The casino was very controversial in its day - both its position and its design - and still arouses conflicting views. It is a love-it or hate-it structure, but either way certainly cannot be ignored. It is likely that in the next few years the world of architecture will take a kinder view of the casino as Niemeyer, who was born in 1907, has been 'rediscovered' by young architects and critics. He is now seen as a founding member of the Modern Movement and in 1998, at the great age of 91, was awarded the British Royal Gold Medal for Architecture, the world's most prestigious prize.

Avenida do Infante

In Avenida do Infante, the other side from Quinta Vigia, a little way downhill towards the city, the **Hospício da Princessa** was endowed by Empress Amelia, as a memory to Princess Marie, as a sanatorium for tuberculosis sufferers. The Brazilian and Swedish emblems can be seen above the entrance: the Brazilian clearly remembers the Empress, the Swedish was for Josephine, Queen of Sweden, the sister of the Empress, who oversaw construction because her sister could not bear to be reminded of her daughter after she had endowed the building. The grounds of the hospital are a lovingly tended garden: the entrance is guarded by an arch formed by two dragon trees.

Continuing along the Avenida, there are some excellent villas in art deco style to the right. To the left is the Savoy Hotel, marking the beginning of Funchal's hotel quarter. Cross the Ribeira Seco - in its steep, wild ravine - to reach the junction with Estrada Monumental. To the right from here, just 100m or so, beyond the Hotel Quinta do Sol, is **Quinta Magnólia**, once a country club for Madeira's British residents, then an expensive hotel and now government owned. The parkland surround the superb mansion has a variety of leisure facilities (swimming pool, tennis courts, even a waymarked nature trail in the Ribeira Seco's ravine) all of which are open to the public. The mansion also houses the island's hotel school and in the restaurant visitors can enjoy food prepared by the students (and be waited on by other students). Nor surprisingly the food is excellent (and also extremely good value). The only drawback is that lunch only is served - for dinner you must go elsewhere.

Bearing left at the junction soon leads to Reid's Hotel. The founding of this, one of the world's great hotels - which, like Raffles in Singapore is known by name to thousands who have never set eyes on it - is the stuff of legend. William Reid was one of twelve children of a Scottish crofter. Born in 1822, William was just 14 when he arrived in Madeira to seek his fortune. He worked as baker's boy, then in the wine trade before meeting William Wilkinson. Together they set up a company finding mansions for rich visitors to the island. With the money he earned Reid bought his own mansions, the better to control the letting. Eventually he bought a small mansion on what he considered the best site on the island and began his own hotel. He died in 1888, three years before the hotel was opened by his sons. The Golden Book of signatures of those who have stayed reads like a list of the world's nobility, its rich and famous. (And, it has to be said, a few of the world's infamous too: as an example Batista stayed after fleeing Cuba in the wake of Castro's revolution). Sir Winston Churchill always enjoyed his stays arriving, as with many celebrity guests, by boat and using the lift to reach the gardens.

Nowadays though, there just aren't enough royals to keep the hotel full, and the rules about dinner jackets and evening dress for dinner have been relaxed in an attempt to reach a wider market. Some will regret the passing of an era, but many others will relish the prospect of a stay. Afternoon tea, something of an island institution, is open to non-residents. It is worth it for the view and the ambience - but do remember to dress smartly.

Heading Back to Zarco - the Harbour and Marina

Walk back through Jardim de Santa Caterina and descend the steps by the chapel to reach Avenida do Mar (now officially called the Avenida das Comunidades Madeirenses, though, perhaps not surprisingly, few use the new name). Ahead, across the water is the huge **Molhe da Pontinha** breakwater. The fort-topped rock towards the landward end is called Loo Rock, a curious name that has stepped through three languages. The Portuguese called it the *Ilhéu* (islet) da Pontinha. The Dutch misunderstood and called it Leeuw (the lion) from which the English called it Loo, the name which has stuck.

Bear left to walk with the busy sea port on your right. To the left is the Marina Shopping Centre which has also recently changed names (from Infante, to the confusion of visitors and the apparent annoyance of locals). To the right now is the new marina, studded with a mix of enthusiasts' boats and downright unaffordable craft. The quays of the marina are colourful with the graffiti of numerous sailors who have used Madeira as the start or finish of Atlantic crossings. Near the marina there are a number of excellent cafes and restaurants, one of the most interesting being the 'floating' restaurant of *The Vagrant*, a 36m (118ft) yacht built in 1941 for the American Horace Vanderbilt. In 1966 the boat was bought by the Beatles, a fact which still encourages pilgrimages. The boat, sold on to the folk singer Donovan and then resold, was wrecked on the Canaries in 1977 and subsequently brought to Funchal. The landlocked boat is surrounded by 'lifeboats' each with its own table.

Close to the boat is a monument to Madeiran emigrants, the island being proud to have 'exported' folk who became rich or famous. Nearby, is a circular tower. The original tower was 30m (100ft) high when erected, in 1798, by the Englishman John Banger not as a lighthouse, as many believe, but as a crane, an intricate system of pulleys helping to load and unload ships. The tower was demolished, amid protests, in 1939 to make way for the new harbour

Funchal

Walking Tour 2

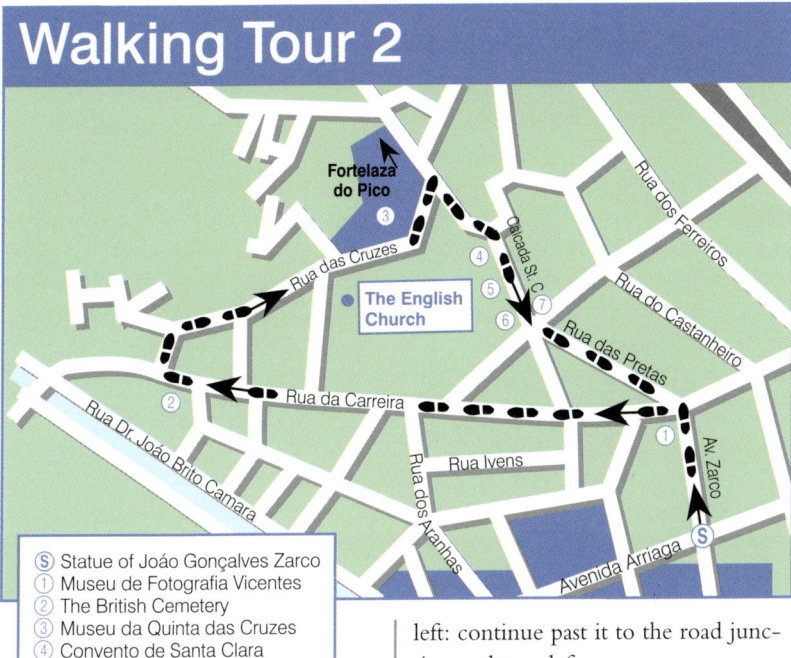

- Ⓢ Statue of João Gonçalves Zarco
- ① Museu de Fotografia Vicentes
- ② The British Cemetery
- ③ Museu da Quinta das Cruzes
- ④ Convento de Santa Clara
- ⑤ Museu Frederico de Freitas
- ⑥ Igreja São Pedro
- ⑦ Museu Municipal
  (part of Palacio de São Pedro)

road, the present tower having been built, with original stones, to appease city folk annoyed by the loss of their landmark.

Now follow Avenida Zarco beside the São Lourenço fortress to return to Zarco's statue.

Walking Tour 2

Zarco to Quinta das Cruzes

From Zarco's statue, head north, away from the sea, along Avenida Zarco, a street that shines yellow in the sun of late summer when the tipuana trees flower. There is a post office on the left: continue past it to the road junction and turn left.

Rua da Carreira

You are now in Rua da Carreira: to the left here - at No. 43, a superb nineteenth century building - is the

Interior of the convent at Santa Clara

47

Sister Maria Clementina, the Reluctant Nun

Maria Clementina was the youngest daughter of a Madeiran family. She was also the loveliest, and by her early teens was renowned as the most beautiful girl on the island. Unfortunately her parents did not share the rest of the island's joy in her appearance and when she was 18 years old she was sent to the Santa Clara convent. The reasons are unclear: some say that Maria's parents were not well off and, having several older daughters, could not afford a dowry for their youngest; others contend that Maria's parents were merely following a Madeiran convention, 'giving' a child to the church being seen as a means of easing a passage to heaven; but most intriguing is the fact that Maria, with her fair skin, blue eyes and brown hair, looked nothing like her sisters and even less like her father - was her parents' antagonism evidence of a secret affair of her mother?

Whatever the reason, Maria joined the convent. That she was a reluctant nun can be seen by her reaction to an edict from the mainland (issued in 1820 when she is believed to have been 19 or 20) that all monastic houses liberate those who had been compelled to take their vows. Maria left immediately and had soon fallen in love with a Portuguese military man (either a soldier or a sailor, the story is vague). The lovers were to be married, but before the ceremony the new edict was revoked. One version of the tale maintains that Maria was ill just before her wedding and that it was postponed for a few weeks and during that time the edict was revoked.

Maria's parents immediately returned her to the convent. Maria's story became one of the scandals of the island and she became a celebrity, many of Madeira's visitors journeying to Santa Clara to talk with her. These conversations were her only companionship and were often supervised by the abbess to ensure that nothing was said that might fuel the fires of scandal. One visitor reporting asking Maria if she was happy and of her replying, 'Yes, very happy' as the abbess smiled, but then leaning forward and whispering 'No, my heart breaks' when the abbess looked away. But happy or sad, Maria never left the convent again, dying there at the age of 65.

Museu de Fotografia Vicentes. Vicente Gomes da Silva was born in Funchal in 1827 and was a teacher as well as an enthusiastic amateur painter. He became interested in the new art of photography and after several years of practising on his family he became Madeira's (and Portugal's) first professional photographer in 1856. The museum is housed in Vicente's original studio, one occupied by his sons and their families until the business closed in 1973, re-opening soon after as a museum. The studio is reached through a delightful courtyard and up a stairway to a wrought-iron clad balcony. The café in the courtyard, its tables shaded by banana trees, is a delightful place for a quiet coffee. The museum's collection includes not only old cameras, but the original screens, painted scenes of Madeira, from which the sitter chose a suitable background. There is also a collection of photographs illustrat-

> ### Sugar Box Furniture
>
> When the Madeiran sugar industry was threatened by cheaper Brazilian sugar, the islanders began to import sugar from Brazil, re-exporting it as 'better quality' Madeiran sugar. The imports arrived in mahogany boxes and were turned into furniture by the enterprising locals. Later the Portuguese East Indian Company brought goods from the Orient in similar hardwood packing cases and these were also used. The resulting sugar-box furniture is much better than would be imagined from the name.

ing the changing face of Funchal and Madeira. The full collection of photos is said to number almost 400,000, many of them so far uncatalogued.

At the entrance to the museum courtyard is the city's English bookshop and The Pátio, with its banana trees. Continue along the road, admiring the wrought iron balconies. The bakery/cake shop at No 75 is renowned for its *bolo de mel*. Further on, to the right, along Rua da Quebra Castas (literally 'break back street') is the **English Church** (officially the Anglican church of the Holy Trinity) a fine neo-classical building built in the 1820s. Legend has it that the design was due, in part at least, from a Portuguese edict that only Roman Catholic churches could look like churches. The bust in the garden is of Phillippa of Lancaster, the daughter of John of Gaunt, who married King João 1 of Portugal in 1386 and was the mother of Prince Henry the Navigator.

Continue along Rua da Carreira, soon reaching the **British Cemetery** on the left. The cemetery was opened in 1764 by the British to allow the burials of Protestants of all nations to be buried. Prior to that date the Portuguese authorities would allow only Catholics to be buried on the island, Protestants being buried at sea - legend having it that they were often thrown off the cliffs to the east of the city. The cemetery is a quiet, rather beautiful place, full of poignant headstones recording the deaths of young people for whom the Madeiran tuberculosis cure came too late. The cemetery is open during daylight hours, but you must ring the bell to summon the caretaker to unlock the gates.

Quinta das Cruzes

Now turn right along Rua da Cruzes, passing beneath the Fortaleza do Pico. There are good views of the sea from the shaded terrace to the left here. Continue beside the wall of Quinta das Cruzes to reach a road junction. Turn left here to reach the entrance of the mansion.

Legend has it that the Quinta das Cruzes (the Mansion of the Crosses) stands on the site of João Gonçalves Zarco's first house at Funchal. It is a wonderful site - Zarco could hardly have chosen a better one - and there is some evidence of very early (perhaps fifteenth century) foundation work, though what we now see is a comprehensive rebuild following earthquake damage to an earlier house in 1748. The house was rebuilt in fine style by the Lomelinos, a Genoese wine trading family, and is furnished in period style. Some of the furniture is local, but there are also pieces by Chippendale and other well-known makers, bought from departing British traders. The quinta is now a museum with some very good collections. The Indian and Chinese art and porcelain was brought back by ships of the Portuguese East Indian Company and includes some exquisite embroidered silk wall hangings and rare pottery dating from the thirteenth century. There are some interesting paintings, including a large view of Funchal, and some costumes and jewellery. The mansion's kitchens have some excellent examples of 'sugar-box furniture'. The mansion's chapel has a good altarpiece by the Portuguese artist Bento Coelho da Silveira.

The gardens of the mansion are as interesting as the interior. They have been designated an Archaeological Park because of the number and quality of the items of stonework which have found a home here. There are very early tombstones and engraved stones from other mansions and churches, including several coats-of-arms. At the centre of the 'Park' is the base of the city's old pillory brought here in 1835. A copy of the original now stands near the Market Hall. The rather grand carving on the pillory suggest it was rather more than a post to which lawbreakers could be tied for ritual humiliation. Probably it was also a symbol of the city's authority.

On the far side of the 'Park' from the mansion, a walkway leads to a beautiful garden. Here are the best historical items - two large carved stone window frames, one carved with man-eating lions (complete with eaten man). The style is known as Manueline as it evolved during the reign of King Manuel I of Portugal. Manuel came to the throne in 1495 which dates the window to the late fifteenth or early sixteenth century. The original site of the windows is unknown, though legend maintains they once adorned a hospital. At the top of the garden is a conservatory where beautiful, shade-loving orchids bloom. It is overtopped by a superb dragon tree.

From the entrance to Quinta das Cruzes, continue steeply uphill - there is no pavement so please be careful - and take the first street on the left to reach a gateway. Beyond is the **Fortaleza do Pico**, still occupied by the military and so closed to visitors. It is occasionally possible to look or go through a small door which allows a close up view of the fortress, and a quick sight of the commanding view it enjoys of the city. The fortress was built in the late sixteenth/early seventeenth century.

Heading back to Zarco

Return downhill and continue along Calçada Santa Clara, soon reaching the **Convento de Santa Clara**, on the right. João Gonçalves Zarco built a chapel here, dedicated to the Immaculate Conception, and his grandchildren founded the convent, for Poor Clare nuns, on the same site. It is said that one of Zarco's grand-daughters was the convent's first abbess. Zarco lived to over 80, long enough to see the establishment, and is buried in the church, beneath the high altar. His tomb is not visible, the impressive tomb from the same period - and which is often mistaken for his - being that of his son-in-law Martin Mendes de Vasconcelos. Two of Zarco's daughters are also buried here. A remnant of Zarco's original chapel can still be seen, though it is now surrounded by later work.

The convent became the richest on Madeira, though it suffered badly at the hands of De Montluc's pirates during the raid of 1566, the nuns fleeing for their lives and the building being stripped of its treasures. Recently, significant finds of *azulejos* from both before and after the raid have been discovered on the church floor, and these are being carefully restored. The walls are completely encased in tiles, some being green, a very rare coloration. The church also has a lovely wooden ceiling. The iron grilles at the back of the church were a nun's sole method of communication with the outside world. Visitors came through a door beyond and could speak through the grill. In the early nineteenth century the nuns were famous for making sugar-based confectionery and flowers from feathers, but so complete was their isolation that these were sold - as souvenirs, or for children - by means of a rotating table which kept the visitor on the other side of a wall and curtain. The convent has beautiful cloisters, in part occupied by a school run by the nuns.

Just beyond the convent, and also on the right, is the **Museu Frederico de Freitas**. The museum is housed in a fine late seventeenth century house built for Count Calçada and comprises the collections of a Madeiran lawyer, Dr Frederico de Freitas, who willed it to the island on his death in 1978. Dr de Freitas was an avid collector, and an eclectic one, his museum being the sort of place where everyone will find something of interest. There is Chinese porcelain, European art work, sacred art and objects, about 2,000 jugs of various types (teapots, milk jugs etc), a marvellous collection of *azulejos*, some very rare, old instruments, Venetian glass and much more. Apart from the azulejos, the prized exhibits are the collection of carved wooden Nativity figures, all from Madeira. The rooms are also beautifully furnished, some with fine English furniture, some with Portuguese antiques, and including some fine examples of sugar-box furniture. The furnishings do full justice to the house, which is itself one of the best exhibits. Later details - the lovely conservatory and art nouveau Winter Garden - enhance the fine style of the house.

The museum also has an exhibition of paintings, drawings and engravings of Madeira, most dating from the nineteenth century. Many of these works were by amateur artists, but they are not without a certain charm and give an idea of how the island looked in its socialite heyday. Pride of place is given to a series of works by Isabella de França whose journal of her honeymoon in Madeira was found accidentally by Dr de Freitas in a secondhand bookshop in London in 1830. The author was Isabella Hurst, daughter of a London architect, who, at the age of 58, married a 50 year-old husband who was London born to an English mother, but had a Madeiran father. Her journal belies her age with its humour and insight, and is a vivid portrait of mid-nineteenth century Madeira.

Continue down the street. To the left is the **Igreja (church) São Pedro**, built at the end of the sixteenth century, though remodelled later. The

51

interior is lined with azulejos, has a floral painted ceiling and a high altar in gilded Baroque style. Opposite the church (with its entrance around the corner in Rua da Mouraria) is the **Museu Municipal** the city's natural history museum, housed in the eighteenth century Palacio de São Pedro. The museum has an aquarium with live specimens of some of the smaller fish and other marine creatures found in the island's waters, and a conventional collection of stuffed creatures. The birds are especially interesting as is the monk seal, one of the world's rarest seals.

Turn left at the bottom of Calçada Santa Clara, then first right along Rua das Pretas. This is 'The Street of Negresses' named because during the time of slavery on Madeira this area of town was a ghetto for black slaves, a curfew preventing them from leaving it during the hours of darkness. The street is now the centre of the Madeiran antique trade. At the end of the road, cross into Avenida Zarco.

Walking Tour 3

Zarco to the Town Hall

On the south-eastern corner of the intersection of Avenida Zarco and Avenida Arriago (at No. 21 Avenida Arriaga) is the Golden Gate Café, one of Funchal's most famous coffee shops. It was once known as the 'Corner of the World' as it was the centre of city life, the meeting and gossiping place for Funchal's folk. Lately the café has lost its position in the social hierarchy, and some of its glamour, but is still a good place for a coffee and a glimpse of local life.

The Cathedral

From Zarco's statue head east along Avenida Arriaga. To the left, **Rua João Tavira** has a delightful pavement, created when the street was made pedestrian only. The mosaic designs of the pavement illustrate Madeiran history - the date of discovery, the caravels of the early settlers and scenes from ancient island life. There is also, incongruously, a bust of Baden-Powell, founder of the Boy Scout movement, the work of the Brazilian born sculptor Ricardo Veloza and erected in early 1998. Just beyond is the *Sé*, **Funchal Cathedral**. The cathedral was begun in 1493, though not finished until 1514, on the instructions of King Manuel I and (hardly surprisingly) is in the style now known as Manueline, a decorated form of European Gothic, though the façade of the building and the tiny windows are a strong echo of Romanesque. The Sé was the first cathedral to be built outside the Portuguese mainland. Externally the decoration that is so distinctive of the Manueline style is best seen at the apse end: look for the twirly pinnacles and towers. Look too for the *azulejos* on the tower's 'roof' which flash dazzlingly in the sun. The clock below the tiles was a gift from Dr Michael Grabham, British born, but a Madeira resident who was an expert on island wildlife.

The cathedral is entered through the beautifully arched doorway in the façade, itself a striking mix of dark basalt and white wash. Above the door is a fine rose window and the symbol of the Order of the Knights of the Cross of which King Manuel was the Grand Master. Inside the Sé the visitor will need to pause for some time: the small windows make it very dark and it will take a while for your eyes to accustom to it. Although the climate is milder in Madeira than on the southern European mainland the congregation was doubtless glad that the windows were minimal on hot summer's days. But even when your eyes have done their best you may well find much of the detailed work difficult to pick out. The lighting is better during services, but that is hardly a reasonable time for sightseeing. The wooden ceiling, in Mujedar style, is in a local hardwood and has some excellent inlaid ivory as well as details in blue and gold. The choir stalls, made of the same wood, also with decorations picked out in blue and gold. The stalls have carvings of apostles and saints under elaborate canopies, the figures dressed in the fashion of the day. Look, too, for the misrichords (which - being beneath choir seats - can be difficult to make out) which have delightful, occasionally *risqué*, carvings of various animals. Finally, be sure to look at the high altar. As with the side altars it is Flemish Baroque, the side panels painted by Flemish and Portuguese artists.

Rua dos Ferreiros

Go along the cathedral's southern (seaward) side - Rua da Sé - to reach the Praça de Colombo, a new, wonderfully airy, square. No. 28 was the site of the mansion a fifteenth century Flemish sugar trader, Jean d'Esmanault (usually called João Esmeraldo, the Portuguese equivalent of his name). It was at this mansion that Christopher Columbus is reputed to have stayed when he visited Madeira to trade sugar. Sadly the mansion was demolished in the nineteenth century after years of neglect. At the square's northern end is the **Centro Museológico do Açucar**, the City of Sugar, which exhibits articles excavated on the site of Jean d'Esmanault's house and the

---

Madeira's Flemish Heritage

At the height of Madeira's sugar boom, a major area of trade was with Flanders. Sometimes sugar consignments were paid for with paintings, sometimes the rich Madeiran sugar merchants commissioned Flemish artists to produce paintings, chiefly with religious themes, which were then donated to island churches. As a result, virtually every church on Madeira acquired a fifteenth or sixteenth century Flemish work. Earlier this century it was realised that priceless art treasures were hanging neglected in tiny churches and it was decided to bring them all to the Old Bishop's Palace. Few of the works have verified attributions, but as an illustration of medieval Flemish sacred art the collection is almost without equal. Some of the works include members of the commissioning family grouped around saints and apostles.

Madeira

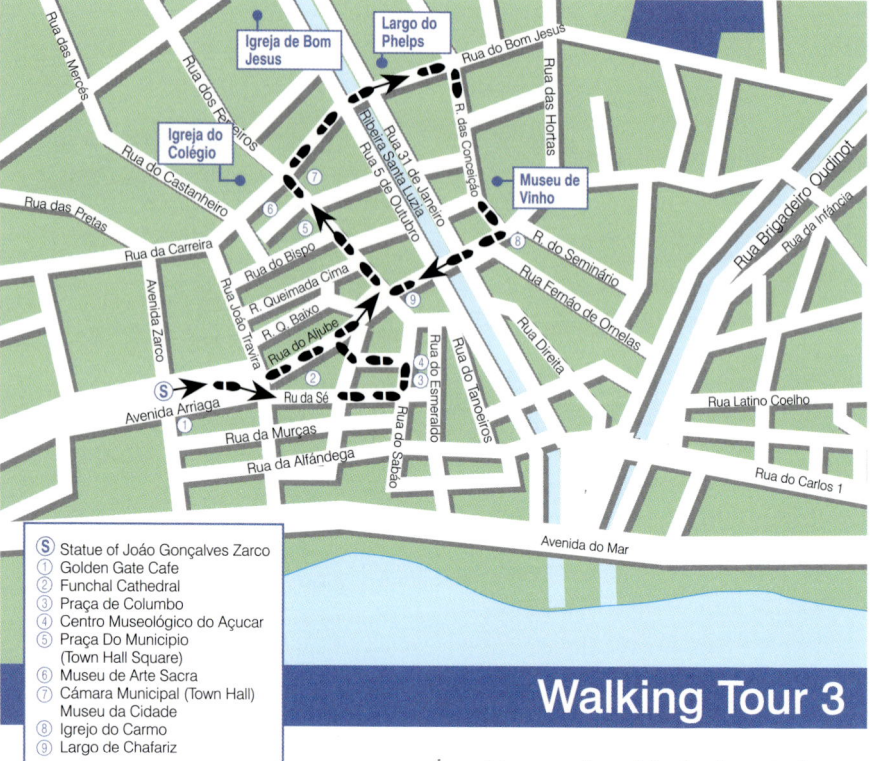

Walking Tour 3

- (S) Statue of João Gonçalves Zarco
- ① Golden Gate Cafe
- ② Funchal Cathedral
- ③ Praça de Columbo
- ④ Centro Museológico do Açucar
- ⑤ Praça Do Município
  (Town Hall Square)
- ⑥ Museu de Arte Sacra
- ⑦ Cámara Municipal (Town Hall)
  Museu da Cidade
- ⑧ Igrejo do Carmo
- ⑨ Largo de Chafariz

surrounding area during construction of the new square. The finds illustrate life in Funchal at during the height of the sugar trade, when Columbus may have been visiting the island.

Return to Rua do Aljube by going along the rear of the cathedral, passing the Penha d'Aguia, a coffee and pastry shop. Turn right to reach Rua das Ferreiros, one of Funchal's smartest shopping streets. Turn left along the street, then second left, along Rua do Bispo, to reach the **Museu de Arte Sacra**, housed in the early seventeenth century (but remodelled extensively in the next century after earthquake damage) Bishop's Palace. The museum has a priceless collection of Flemish paintings and other works of great beauty and interest. Arguably the finest is the ornate gilded silver processional cross given to Funchal cathedral in 1528 by King Manuel I.

Praça do Município

Return to Rua das Ferreiros and continue along it for a few steps to reach **Praça do Município** (Town Hall Square), the best of all the city's squares. The centre of the square is paved with dark basalt and white marble, the pattern of semi-circles said to represent the scales of a fish. At the centre is a fountain with a tall central pillar topped by an armillary (a celestial globe). Cobbled streets surround the central square, and they are surrounded in turn by a series of marvellous Baroque buildings. On

The tower of Funchal Cathedral

the square's southern (south-eastern to be precise) edge is the Bishop's Palace (Museum of Sacred Art). Across from the palace is the **Igreja do Colégio** - the Collegiate Church of St John the Evangelist - built by the Jesuits in 1629. The Jesuits arrived on Madeira in 1566 in the wake of the raid by the French pirate De Montluc (they actually came with a fleet of ships carrying soldiers, sent by the king to repel the pirate attack, but by the time the ships arrived De Montluc had long gone). The Jesuits were a considerable help to the islanders, offering comfort to those traumatised by the raid and helping to rebuild the island's trade: they are credited with having introduced the Sercial and Verdelho grapes to Madeira. The islanders helped to establish a Jesuit college as a mark of thanks, though it was a relatively short-lived venture: in 1760 the Portuguese expelled the Order from the country, fearing its power. The expulsion included Madeira, the church and the college beside it falling into disrepair. It became a military barracks, finally being taken over by Madeira's University of which it now forms part. The church, with its imposing façade, its niches holding statues of saints.(St Ignatius de Loyola, the founder of the Jesuit Order is in the bottom, left-hand niche) has a superb collection of *azulejos*. There are also some good paintings and a delightful *trompe l'œil* ceiling.

At the western end (true north-east) is the equally attractive **Câmara Municipal**, the Town Hall. Look for the Madeiran coat-of-arms carved into the stonework of the façade: it consists of five sugar loaves - Madeira's sugar was poured into a clay cones to prepare it for export as 'sugar loaves' - and four grapes, reflecting the island's trading heritage. The Câmara dates from 1758, and was built (in gracious style) for the island's then richest inhabitant, Count João José de Carvalhal. The count kept his horses and wine barrels on the ground floor, and his family on the first floor. The tower was a look-out for the Count, helping him spot arriving ships early and so beat his rivals to the port. (Such towers are actually a tradition in Madeira, the earliest ones - of which a good example can be seen at the other end of the square - having been raised to spot pirate, rather than trading, ships). The mansion stayed in the family hands until the end of the nineteenth century when it became the Town Hall. During working hours the building's inner courtyard is open to visitors. Here the fish scale paving of the square is repeated, the lower walls are tiled with *azulejos*, and there is a superb fountain with a statue of Leda and the Swan. The Town Hall is also home to the **Museu da Cidade** (city museum) which traces the history of Madeira and Funchal. The museum, on the building's first floor, uses a timeline to trace the island's history, illustrated with some interesting snippets and objects. It notes, for instance, that the first children born on Madeira were twins, a boy and a girl who were christened (what else?) Adam and Eve. There are also some clay sugar loaf moulds and João Gonçalves Zarco's sword.

Opposite the Colégio is the **Museum of Sacred Art** - there is another entrance on the square side, the square being closed on its fourth side by shops and the Bar O Leque, an excellent coffee shop.

Heading back to Zarco

Leave Praça do Município along the Town Hall's northern side, crossing Rua 5 de Outubro. To the left along this road is the **Museu do Vinho**, a museum housed in the offices of the Madeiran Wine Institute which guarantees the quality of all the island's wine.

The museum explores the history of the industry and of winemaking.

Continue ahead, crossing a bridge over the Ribeira de Santa Luzia. Funchal's rivers have a somewhat sorry history, having for years been used as a rubbish dump, then having their banks concreted. Today they are filled with bougainvillaea which makes them glorious ribbons of colour and hides the worst excesses. But though the concreting was an undignified process for proud rivers it was necessary to control occasionally devastating floods. In 1803 flooding of the Santa Luzia drowned about 600 people. Legend has it that one wealthy English trader was having a dinner party for many guests when the river flooded. So ferocious was the water, and so rapid the rise that the house was carried away in its entirety, the lights still blazing as it sank in the harbour with the loss of hosts and all the guests.

It seems a very unlikely tale, but the floodwaters of Funchal's rivers were legendary, and the damage they wreaked undoubtedly horrific. The new channels have reduced, though not eliminated, the problem. Cross the river and continue along Rua do Bom Jesus, soon reaching the church of the name, a fine seventeenth century building, on the left. After two centuries as a nunnery, the church became a home for impoverished widows and abandoned wives. It is now a nunnery again, but only for lay nuns.

Turn right just after, following **Rua da Conceição**, a delightful narrow lane in which some of Funchal's oldest buildings stand. Nos. 49-53 have been recently restored and with their superb balconies and tower are a delight.

At the bottom of the street, to the left, is the **Igreja do Carmo**, a seventeenth century Carmelite church. The church has some good modern azulejos and the tombs of Counts of Carvalhal, mounted on the backs of lions.

Turn right into **Largo do Phelps**, a small square (if a square can be three-sided!) named for Elizabeth Phelps, the daughter of a wine merchant, who started the Madeiran embroidery 'industry'. Exiting the little square to the left is Rua Fernão de Ornelas, one of Funchal's main shopping streets, a fascinating mix of modern supermarkets and old shops, selling everything from *objets d'art* to furniture, many of the shops (and some of the stocks) seemingly as old as the buildings themselves.

Cross the river again to reach the end of Rua do Betencourt and Largo de Chafariz, a pretty little square. To the right here is the *Bazar do Povo*, literally the Pauper's Bazaar, a shopping area where the poor of Funchal could once find anything they wanted, and all at rock-bottom prices. The spirit of the bazaar lives on, making the area a fascinating place to visit. In Rua do Aljube, to the left are numerous flower stalls and the occasional seller of *barretes de lã*, the famous Madeiran woollen hat. These multi-coloured hats, complete with ear flaps and an eccentric top-knot bottle are the ideal souvenir. Continue along Rua do Aljube to return to Zarco.

Walking Tour 4

Zarco to the Old Town

From Zarco's statue follow Avenida Zarco towards the sea, with the Forteleza de São Lourenço on your

Madeiran Embroidery

It is known that the womenfolk of Madeira - particularly the nuns - had been embroidering clothing and table decorations from the sixteenth century, but the credit for starting the industry which is now such a feature of the island is usually given to Elizabeth Phelps. Miss Phelps, Bella to her friends, was the unmarried daughter of Joseph Phelps, an English wine trader. The Phelps family had a history of missionary work and Bella, a delicate lady, helped at the convent of Santa Clara, and also at an orphanage in Santana.

Bella was active in the 1840s when cholera swept the island killing thousands and, soon after, when mildew destroyed the vines. Appalled by the poverty and suffering these events caused, Bella taught her charges to embroider cotton and on one of her regular visits to London took samples of their work for sale. Some samples reached Queen Victoria's court where the ladies bought them with enthusiasm and clamoured for more. In 1851 Bella exhibited Madeiran embroidery at London's Great Exhibition and, soon, no English bride could contemplate marriage without Madeiran embroidery forming part of her gown or trousseau, and no tea party in an elegant town house or stately home could take place without a table cloth and doilies from the island. By 1862 there were 10,000 embroiderers on the island, not only women, but children and men too. Indeed, whole families were sometimes employed to make larger pieces such as table cloths. Most embroidery shops on the island will tell you the story (probably apocryphal, but feasible enough to be true) about the family working on a large tablecloth, mother and daughters at one end, father and sons at the other who, when they met in the middle, discovered they had been working on opposite sides of the cloth.

By 1880 the fashion for Madeiran embroidery had declined in Britain, but the German Otto Von Streit revitalised the industry. He introduced a machine, the máquina de picotar, which printed the design on to the cloth, so avoiding the need for pre-stitching and speeding the process. More cleverly he also sought, and found, new markets for the finished articles. Today Von Streit's machine is still used at the first stage of production in the factory, though the bordadeiras (embroiderers) are still home-workers. They are now almost exclusively women, usually older women earning extra money by doing some embroidery as a relaxation between chores and other work: few are full time embroiderers. Young girls pick up the skills from their mothers, but children below the age of 14 are unable to become registered workers and, therefore, to be paid. All workers are paid by the stitch, though the quality of the work is also a factor. It is estimated that today about 10,000 people are involved in the industry, almost the same number as in Elizabeth Phelps' time.

At several places in Madeira and especially in Funchal, visitors will see embroidery 'factories' advertised. The name is somewhat misleading. Embroidery remains a cottage industry, the factory preparing the cloth and thread for the bordadeiras and marketing the finished products. Originally Madeiran embroidery used only white thread on white cotton, but modern works involve colours and a broader range of materials, including silk. Embroidery is a wonderful souvenir of a visit - and the visitor can hardly avoid seeing it, not only on street stalls, but on postcards and even occasionally on stamps - but is not cheap. Though this is no surprise in view of the labour-intensive nature of the manufacture and the quality of the work, it makes finding the genuine article worth the time spent.

All official bordadeiras must be registered with IBTAM, the Instituto de Bordados, Tapeçária e Artesanato (Institute of Embroidery, Tapestry and Handicrafts) and to be sure of buying the genuine product look for the IBTAM seal. Funchal has an IBTAM centre with authentic work.

right. Turn left along Avenida do Mar. Just beyond the statue (on the left) of Pope John Paul II, another work by Ricardo Veloza, sculpted to commemorate the Pope's visit to Madeira in 1991, is the **Alfândega**, the Old Customs House, built in the 1470s, making it one of the oldest buildings on the island. The Customs House was badly damaged in the earthquake of 1748 and rebuilt, and has been extended and remodelled several times since. It is now the seat of the regional parliament, the parliament chamber on the seaward side, and the waterfall fountain being the latest additions. Most Madeirans believe the additions are completely out-of-character, but that seems a little harsh. However, to see the best of the building, turn up the plaza you have crossed to reach the House, and turn first right. There, in Rua da Alfândega, is the Manueline doorway of the original house, the oldest surviving section and one of the best examples of the type of the island. Visitors are rarely allowed into the Alfândega, but if the opportunity arises, take it: on the first floor is one of the finest carved-wood ceilings in Portugal and the tallest pottery vase in the world, a 5.3m (17.5ft) creation by potters from Portugal and Brazil. Opposite the Alfândega the onion-topped coffee kiosk is the best of those on the seafront.

Continue along Avenida do Mar, soon reaching the **Praça da Autonomia**, the square's name commemorating the award of autonomy to Madeira in the wake of the 1974 Portuguese revolution. The monument - the *Monumento a Autonomia*, marooned by roads - is an extraordinary, but powerful, work, depicting a woman emerging from a block of bronze, a symbolic prison, her head held aloft in triumph. At the northern edge is a replica of the old city pillory (*pelourinho*) whose original base is the centrepiece of Quinta das Cruze's Archaeological Park.

Walk through the square, away from the sea, and bear right, crossing the Ribeira de João Gomes to reach the **Mercado dos Lavradores**, the Market Hall, one of the liveliest places in Funchal. It should not be missed for the flower sellers in traditional Madeiran dress at the entrance, and for the assault on the senses the stalls offer - every colour that can be conceived, a constant barrage of noise and an array of smells that threatens to overload the nostrils completely.

The Hall was built in the late 1930s by Edmundo Tavares one of the leading Portuguese architects of the time. He created an art deco building on two levels around a central courtyard, its distinctly Madeiran touches including the use of *azulejos*, and a reminder of the old watch towers for early warning of pirate attacks. Beyond the flower sellers - who specialise in orchids and will pack for homeward transport by plane if you wish - are stalls of fruit and vegetables, some of the produce laid out in traditional wicker baskets, together with fresh and dried herbs, fresh bread, wine, craftwork (including leather goods and, of course, wickerwork) and much else besides. The best time to visit - for the range and quantity of goods on offer - is Friday and Saturday when the farmers from outlying parts of Madeira arrive. But there is really no bad time to come.

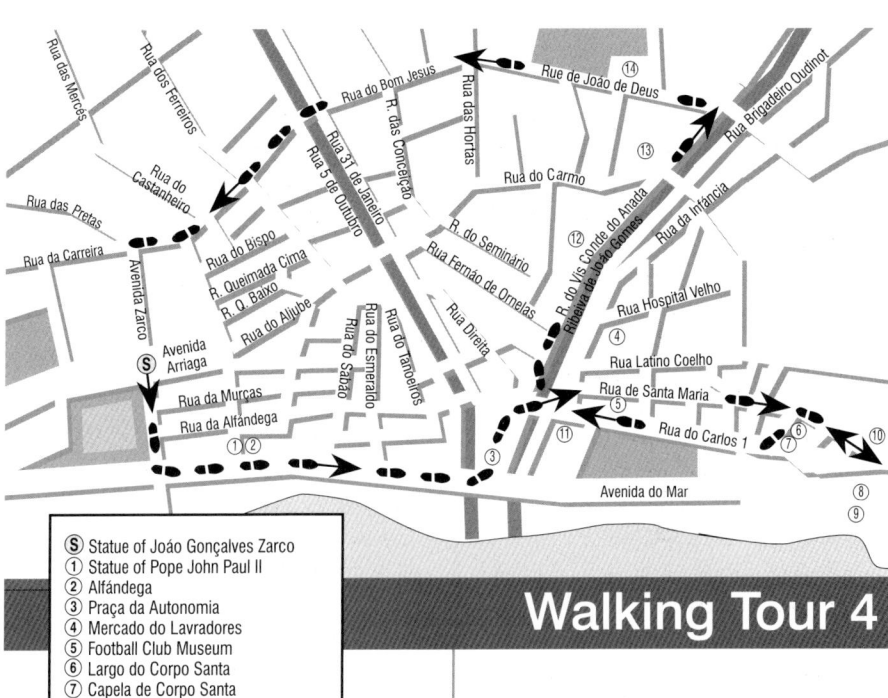

Funchal

S Statue of João Gonçalves Zarco
① Statue of Pope John Paul II
② Alfándega
③ Praça da Autonomia
④ Mercado do Lavradores
⑤ Football Club Museum
⑥ Largo do Corpo Santa
⑦ Capela de Corpo Santa
⑧ Fortaleza de São Tiago,
⑨ Museu de Arte Contemporánea Praia da Barreirinta
⑩ Igreja de Santa Maria Maior
⑪ Museu de Electicidade
⑫ Patricio & Gouveia
⑬ Museu do Bordada e do Artesanato
⑭ Museu Franco

Walking Tour 4

Next to the Market Hall (part of the same complex) is the fish market, an even more emphatic attack on the nostrils. Here slabs cut from tuna lie beside fish with beautiful colour patterns and unfamiliar names. Adventurous visitors who try the local fish restaurants will recognise *espada*, the sinister-looking, long and narrow black fish with razor-sharp teeth. To enjoy the sights and smells of the fish market come early. As elsewhere, Madeira's fishing boats land their catches in the small hours and most of the fish has gone by mid/late morning.

To the south of the market - just across from Praça da Autonomia - is the **Museu de Electricidade**, a museum exploring the history of power production on the island housed in a building on an old power station. The museum is very modern and far more interesting than the subject might imply. Across the street and right from the museum's entrance, the committed football fan might enjoy the Museum of the Club Sporting Maritimo, Funchal, one of the island's foremost football teams. The museum houses the club's phenomenal collection of trophies, medals and pennants. CSM were Portuguese champions in 1926 and are looking to be in European competition within a few years.

Between the market and the electricity museum is Rua de Santa Maria - claimed to be the oldest street in Funchal - in which there are some

Lido Funchal

excellent restaurants. Follow the street into Largo do Corpo Santo, a lovely old cobbled square with several pleasant cafés and, as a contrast, some work-based buildings. Step right here to reach the chapel of the name. **Capela de Corpo Santo** is a very old chapel, dating from the Manueline period. It was built by the fishermen of Funchal, and is still looked after by their successors. With its neat little basalt bell-tower the chapel is delightful.

Pass to the right of the chapel, following a narrow alleyway between simple, single-storeyed houses to reach the **Fortaleza de São Tiago**. The Fortress of St John was built in 1614, then extended in the eighteenth century. With its round towers and curiously coloured walls it is very picturesque. It is claimed to be one of the finest castles of its type in Portugal. After many years of occupation by the military it is now the home of Madeira's **Museu de Arte Contemporânea** (Museum of Contemporary Art), a small collection of work by Portuguese artists who have been active from the 1960s to the present day. Below the fortress the Praia da Barreirinha is a small beach used mostly by the inhabitants of the old town. It is reached by a lift that descends through the cliff (the equivalent of a five-storey drop). In addition to the beach (of pebbles) the lift reaches sunbathing terraces, changing rooms and cafes. There is also a paddling pool for younger visitors.

Continue along Rua de Santa Maria (which the alley beside the Corpo Santo chapel meets close to Fortaleza São Tiago) to reach **Igreja de Santa Maria Maior**, a fine church occasionally called the Igreja do Socorro, the Church of Salvation, as it stands on the burial site of victims of Black Death, which struck the island in 1523. The first church was raised in thanks by those who survived. The present church, in Baroque style, is eighteenth century. Inside is a shrine to St James the Younger who, the Madeirans believed, interceded on their behalf to halt the spread of the Plague.

Heading back to Zarco

From the church, return along Rua de Santa Maria to Largo do Corpo Santo, steeping left there to reach Rua Dom Carlos I, another very ancient cobbled street of single-storey houses, many of them the workshops of furniture makers and other craftworkers. Turn left to reach the market, and bear left there to cross the river. Ahead in Rua Fernao de Ornelas (just a few shops) Severa is Funchal's cheapest coffee shop. Turn right along Rua do Visconde do Anadia, beside the river. In this street is **Patricio & Gouveia**, a shop selling embroidery, wine and other souvenirs, but in which all aspects of the production of embroidery can be seen. Further on is the **Museu do Bordada e do Artesanto** - more commonly called the **IBTAM** building - on the left. The Institute governs the production of handicrafts on Madeira, and the building includes a museum to some of the finest embroidery and tapestry, much of it from the end of the nineteenth/early twentieth centuries. Some of the work is exquisite, showing an ability which borders on genius. There are also pieces by more modern workers, including the tapestry artist Gino Ormolu. His vast *Allegory of Madeira*, executed by a team of schoolgirls (who made seven million stitches between 1958 and 1961) greets visitors. The museum also has an excellent collection of traditional Madeiran costumes.

Continue along Rua do Visconde do Anadia, turning first left along Rua de João de Deus to reach the **Museu Franco**, on the right. The museum, housed in an interesting, church-like, building, is dedicated to the work of the artist and brothers Henrique and Francisco Franco de Sousa. The brothers were Madeiran, but spent most of their lives in Lisbon, from where they travelled to visit the pioneers of the early twentieth century's artistic revolution, being friends with Picasso and Modigliani. Henrique, the elder brother (born in 1883: he died in 1961) was a painter whose work shows the influences of Cezanne, Van Gogh and, most clearly, Gauguin. He was an excellent portrait painter, particularly of the poorer farming folk of Madeira. His younger brother Francisco (1885-1955), a sculptor, is the more famous, though this is, in part at least, due to his works being seen in prominent sites. In Funchal his Sower in Santa Caterina Park and his statue of Zarco are well-known landmarks. The museum has an excellent collection of the work of both brothers and should be on the itinerary of all art lovers.

Continue along Rua João de Deus, then Rua Bom Jesus, crossing Ribeira de Santa Luzia to reach Praça do Muncípio. Now go along Rua Câmara Pestana and turn left along Avenida Zarco.

Places to Visit

Fortress (or Palace) of São Lourenço
Avenida Zarco
Open: Guided tours on Wed at 10am, Fri at 3pm and Sat at 10am and 11am.
☎ 202530

Adegas de São Francisco (Madeira Wine Company)
Avenida Arriaga, 28
Open: All year, Mon-Fri 9.30am-6pm, Sat 10am-1pm.
Guided tours at 10.30am, 2.30pm, 3.30pm and 4.30pm on Mon-Fri, 11am on Sat.
☎ 223065

Columbus Museum
Diogos Wine Shop
Avenida Arriaga, 48
Open: All year, Mon-Fri 10am-1pm, 3-7pm; Sat 9.30am-1pm.
☎ 233357

Museu de Fotografia Vicentes (Photography Museum)
Rua da Carreira, 43
Open: All year, Mon-Fri 10am-12.30pm, 2-5pm.
☎ 225050

Quinta das Cruzes
Calçada do Pico, 1
Open: All year, Tue-Sat 10am-12.30pm, 2-5.30pm, Sun 10am-1pm.
☎ 740670

Convento de Santa Clara
Calçada Santa Clara
Open: All year, daily 9am-12noon, 3-6pm. Ring the bell if the door is closed. Closed during services. There is no admission fee, but a donation is appreciated.
Contact the Funchal Tourist Office - there is no telephone number for the convent.

Museu Frederico de Freitas
Calçada de Santa Clara
Open: All year, Tue-Sat 10am-12.30pm, 2-5.30pm, Sun 10am-12.30pm.
☎ 220578

Museu Municipal (Natural History Museum and Aquarium)
Rua da Mouraria, 31
Open: All year, Tue-Fri 10am-6pm, Sat, Sun and Public Holidays 12noon-6pm. ☎ 229761

Centro Museológico do Açucar (City of Sugar Museum)
Praça Colombo, 5
Open: All year, Mon-Fri 10am-12.30pm, 2-6pm.
☎ 236910

Museu de Arte Sacra (Museum of Sacred Art)
Rua do Bispo, 21
Open: All year, Tue-Sat 10am-12.30pm, 2.30-6pm, Sun 10am-1pm.
☎ 228900

Museu de Cidade (City Museum)
Town Hall
Praça do Município
Open: Mon-Fri 9am-12.30pm, 2-5.30pm.
☎ 220064

Museu do Vinho
Rua 5 de Outubro, 78
Open: All year, Mon-Fri 9.30am-6pm, Sat 9am-1pm.
☎ 204600

Mercado dos Lavradores (Market Hall)
Largo dos Lavradores
Open: All year, Mon 7am-2pm, Tue-Thur and Sat 7am-4pm, Fri 7am-8pm.
☎ 214080

Museu de Electricidade
Rua Casa da Luz, 2 (this road is the first few steps of Rua Dom Carlos I)
Open: All year, daily except Mon. 10am-12.30pm, 2-6pm
☎ 211480

Museu de Club Sporting Maritimo
Rua Dom Carlos I, 14
Open: All year, Mon-Fri 9am-6pm.
No telephone.

Museu de Arte Contemporânea
Forteleza de São Tiago
Open: All year, Mon-Sat 10am-12.30pm, 2-5.30pm.
☎ 213340

Patricio & Gouveia
Rua do Visconde do Anadia, 33
Open: All year, factory: Mon-Fri 9am-1pm and 2-6pm
shop: Mon-Fri 3-6pm, Sat 9.30am-12noon.
☎ 222928

Museu do Bordado e do Artesanto (IBTAM Institute/ Embroidery and Craft Museum)
Rua do Visconde do Anadia, 44
Open: All year, Mon-Fri 10am-12.30pm, 2-5.30pm.
☎ 223141

Museu Franco
Rua do João de Deus, 13
Open: All year, Mon-Fri 10am-12.30pm, 2-6pm.
☎ 230633

2. Around Funchal

Close to Funchal there are several sites which are worth visiting but which do not require visitors to have their own transport because they are just a short taxi or bus ride away. In this chapter we explore these sites.

Jardim Botânico

The Quinta do Bom Successo (Good Fortune Estate), a short (about 3.5km - 2 miles) distance to the north-east of the centre of Funchal, was owned by the Reid family - who also owned Reid's Hotel - and laid out as gardens for their enjoyment. In 1952 the estate was given to Madeira and, a few years later, was opened to the public. For the gardener or plant lover the garden is one of the great highlights of a trip to the island, vying with Blandy's and the Monte Tropical Garden (see below) for the title of the very best.

The garden occupies a terraced hillside which rises 150m (almost 500ft) to a height of about 350m (1,150ft) above sea level, a climb which is surprisingly untaxing, probably because there is so much to enjoy that you barely notice the exertion. The trees and shrubs are arranged geographically, those closest

Opposite: Mergulho Garajau

to the old family mansion being indigenous Madeiran species, and some from nearby island groups - the Canaries, the Azores and the Cape Verde Islands. Elsewhere there is a section for tropical plants and a fine tree plantation. Interspersed between these main areas, and within them, are flower beds and a superb collection of cacti. In the immediate vicinity of the mansion there is a good collection of orchids.

At the top of the garden there is a famous *miradouro* (viewpoint) of Funchal and the bay, looking out over the new expressway as it crosses a bridge which is claimed to be the highest in Europe. The road was much needed and the bridge is superb engineering, but it hardly enhances the view. There are also magnificent views from the bar/cafe closer to mansion level. Close to the cafe peacocks wander about and there are ponds in which frogs croak noisily.

The old Reid mansion has now been converted into a museum of Madeira's natural history with collections of fossils, insects, spiders, fish, plants and birds, those these have been sadly neglected and are nowhere near as good as those Funchal's museum.

At the bottom of the Gardens there is a connection to the **Jardim de Loiros** which has a collection of aviaries housing parrots, cockatoos, macaws and parakeets and similar species.

Down the road from the Botanical Gardens /Jardim de Loiros is the **Jardim Orquídea**, a commercial orchid nursery. Some of the plants grown here are among the rarest orchids in the world requiring their early years to be spent in jars subject to strict environmental control. During the orchid flowering period (late November to early April) the garden is marvellous place where visitors can not only enjoy the sights and scents of a variety of orchids - some so breathtakingly beautiful and delicate that it seems they cannot be real - but also gain an insight into the methods of growing and packaging of the flowers for export. The latter aspects of orchid production and sale can still be explored during the remainder of the year, but the number of flowers in bloom is then severely limited.

Quinta Boa Vista

To the south of the Jardim Botânico lies Quinta Boa Vista. This estate actually lies a short distance to the north-east of Funchal's old town, but to reach it from there requires a long walk: it is better to make a specific journey. The mansion is the home of the ex-British consul to Madeira, Sir Cecil Garton and his wife Betty, explaining the occasionally seen name of Garton Greenhouse for the site. Betty Garton has an international reputation as a grower of orchids and it is orchids for which the gardens of the mansion are famous, though the terraces are also home to numerous sub-tropical species. As at the Jardim Orquídea, the orchids flower only from late November to early April, but here the rest of the garden makes a visit at any time of year worthwhile. Again as at Jardim Orquídea, the Quinta Boa Vista orchids can be bought.

Quinta do Palheiro Ferreiro (Blandy's Garden)

Also north-east of Funchal, about 9.5km (6 miles) from the city centre on the road to Camacha (ER 102) is the Quinta do Palheiro Ferreiro, the second (of two) candidates for the title of finest garden on Madeira. The estate here was owned by the Count of Carvalhal who built a mansion in the late nineteenth century and, it is said, used the grounds for private hunting. After a visit to England he returned full of enthusiasm for landscaping the estate and much of the work on the garden dates from this era. In the main it was carried out by a French landscape gardener. In 1885 the Blandy family bought the estate, built a mansion for themselves and continued the process of turning the estate into a magnificent garden. One of the Blandy owners married a South African who brought many plants from her nature land, adding an African flavour to the tropical and European scene.

The Blandy's house is still occupied and is not open to the public: the car park for the gardens lies close to it. Nearby is the first of several areas planted with araucaria, Himalayan pine and magnolia. Elsewhere, these sub-tropical (and other, tropical) trees are interspersed with beech, oak and chestnut planted by the Blandy family as a reminder of their homeland. In front of the Blandy house is a sunken garden with salvias and verbenas and other, more exotic, plants, and a more formal section of garden with paths criss-crossing between areas planted with so many different species that to even attempt a description would be to fail.

Bearing left, the visitor crosses a levada to reach the original landscaping of the Counts of Carvalhal. To the right is the old house reached by an avenue of plane trees. The house - fronted by holm oaks - has been unoccupied for many years: to the left is the Count's family chapel, a neat Baroque building. Legend has it that the Count had the chapel (the Capela São João) built at this spot so that he could watch the priest celebrating Mass without the need to leave his comfortable seat on the mansion's verandah. Behind the old house there are extensive fish ponds, in front of which are a splendid array of flower beds and borders, and a fruit garden. Beyond is the Jardim de Senhora (Lady's Garden), arguably the most peaceful spot on the estate. The topiary hedges are of an Australian relative to the box, and are typical of French (and Italian) landscaping, the form accentuating formal geometrical patterns, as opposed to the more natural form of an English garden. One of the highlights of the Lady's Garden is the *Datura candida*, white thornapple, with its large funnel-shaped flowers. Beyond the Lady's Garden is another sunken garden with ponds - if you arrive early in the morning and hurry to the ponds you will hear a 'dawn chorus' of frogs.. From the edge of this garden there is a splendid view south across the neighbouring golf course towards the coast and, to the right, towards Funchal.

The English style of landscape gardening is best seen in an area called Inferno, where a natural hollow has been filled with giant ferns and other shade-loving species. Close by - head towards the Blandy house - are a number of South African proteas.

Monte

To the north of Funchal, about 6km (4 miles) distant, but rising to around 600m (2,000ft) lies the village of Monte. Until 1939 visitors from Funchal could take a funicular (rack and pinion) railway to the village. The railway was a superb piece of engineering, as the, now ivory-clad, bridges passed on any journey to Monte suggest,. It must also have offered magnificent views, the 20 minute ride passing fine mansions and gardens, and offering a widening panorama of the coast. But in 1919 one of the steam engines exploded, killing four passengers. The line almost immediately went into decline, increasingly labelled as untrustworthy by visitors and locals alike. The railway struggled on until 1939, but then another, thankfully more minor, accident forced its closure. The lines were ripped up and sold to the mainland, and today visitors must use a bus or taxi - or put their heads down for a long and exhausting walk.

The main village square, the **Largo da Fonte**, where visitors are dropped by coaches and taxis lies a short distance from the church. Here there is a fine fountain whose statue of the Virgin is also considered to be sacred. As a result the fountain is often surrounded by flowers and votive offerings. The square also has stalls selling souvenirs, a good café an, invariably, an accordion player. To reach the village church from the square follow either of the two paths.

The Church of **Nossa Senhora do Monte** has a distinctive façade, its symmetrical towers being picked out easily from Funchal. The first chapel on the site is claimed to have been built by Adam and Eve Gonçalves Ferreiro, the twin children who were the first to have been born on the island, though some experts doubt this claim. The present church dates from 1818, the earlier church having been destroyed in the earthquake of 1748.

The story of the founding by the first true Madeirans is disputed by an old legend. This claims that a local girl had visions of the Virgin Mary near Terreiro da Luta, but that her parents did not believe her when she told them. One day when the girl went off to talk to the Virgin her disbelieving father followed her. He did not see the Virgin, but where he lay in hiding to watch his daughter he found a statue of the Madonna. This statue, revered as a worker of miracles, is still in the church which was built to house it: it is a small statue, kept in a silver shrine on the high altar. On the left of the entrance a fine azulejo depicts the girl and her vision and the doubting father.

Also within the church is the tomb of the last of the Habsburgs, the Emperors of Austro-Hungary. When the Habsburg Empire was dismantled at the end of the 1914-18 war, Karl von Habsburg was forced into exile, eventually arriving on Madeira in 1921 with his wife and five children. The family took up residence in Quinta Gordon, close to the church in Monte. Karl von

The Palace Tropical Gardens at Monte

Habsburg was a young man, only 35, but he was also a sick one, the decision to move to Madeira being taken on medical grounds, as well as for the fact that the island was well removed from mainland Europe. Unfortunately the famed Madeiran climate did not help the deposed emperor and he died within six months of his arrival. He is buried in a simple black sarcophagus adorned with a single crucifix. His wife and children left Madeira: on her death the Empress Zita Bourbon-Parma was buried in Vienna. There have been attempts to return the emperor to lie beside her, but these have all failed.

The church is reached by 70 or so steep steps. As you descend them, it is worth considering the pilgrims at Madeira's major religious festival who climb to the church on their knees. The festival takes place on the Feast of the Assumption (15 August) and is dedicated to Our Lady of Monte. In 1803 when the rivers in Funchal broke

The World's largest vase at the Palace Tropical Gardns

Around Funchal

Curral Das Freiras

The Monte Toboggans

It is said that an Englishman invented the bullock-drawn sled in about 1850 as a means of transport for his wife around Funchal after the city's hammock carriers had declined to carry her again on account of her bulk. The story is probably apocryphal, certainly chauvinistic and even historically dubious, but may have an element of truth. It is likely that bullock sleds were in use on the island before the nineteenth century, they are, after all, a fairly well-established means of transport in hilly country with few roads. But as Funchal's streets were all cobbled, and the cobbles did not agree with the thin-wheeled transport of the day, it would be most unlikely that sleds were not used in the city. Certainly bullock-drawn sleds were used in Funchal until fairly recent times, eventually being banned as they held up the traffic.

In about 1960 sleds - now more usually referred to as toboggans - began to be used by enterprising Madeirans to transport tourist from Monte to Funchal. But these sled did not need bullocks, gravity providing the motive power. The tourists sat in a wicker chair mounted on wooden sleds which ran easily over the cobbles on the descent. The speed of descent was controlled by two men who then laboured back up the hill to repeat the trip. The toboggan men are still providing the rides for tourists, the descent being one of the highlights of a visit to Madeira. In some ways the ride has changed little over the 40 or so years since it began - the toboggans (carro de cesto) are still much the same and the two controllers (carreiros) still wear the traditional uniform of white trousers, white shirt and straw hat (a uniform they are required to wear by law). But there are differences - some section of the cobbled road have been tarmaced, which might be seen as a bonus for the sled men but in fact slows the toboggans so that they now push as often as they pull back to brake, and a lorry takes toboggan and carreiros back to Monte, a very real bonus.

The full ride - the Full Monte - takes you from Monte to the southern end of Rua do Comboio from where it is only a few minutes walk to Praça do Município. This journey of about 4km (2.5 miles) takes about 20 minutes, a reasonable walking speed, with the faster sections being traversed at up to 10kph (6mph, about jogging speed). A shorter trip ends at Livramento (about 2km - 1.25 miles - from Monte). Add the cost of the ride to the inevitable tip for the carreiros, and extra for the photo inevitably taken by someone along the way and offered at an inflated price at the bottom, and the ride is definitely not cheap - but what price can be set on romance and this is without doubt the most romantic trip on the island.

their banks and hundreds were drowned the city folk came to Monte to pray for the rain, which had swollen the rivers, to stop. It did and since that time Our Lady of Monte has been the island's patron saint. The festival is a wonderfully colourful affair with folk gathering from all over the island for a celebration which includes music and dancing, and fireworks as well as a religious procession to the church and a Mass.

At the base of the steps are the Monte toboggan men, but first turn left to reach (after about 300m) the **Jardim do Monte Palace**, the Monte Palace Tropical Garden, a wonderful place but one whose exploration requires a good deal of climbing. The garden once belonged to a local hotel, but became badly neglected. It was then bought by José Berardo, a Madeiran who made a fortune in South Africa by inventing a system which extracted gold from the discarded spoil heaps of gold mines. He returned to Madeira, bought the garden and re-established it as one of the island's prime sites. As well as Madeiran species of plants, including many orchids, Berardo also introduced South African species including cycads, the huge palm-like ferns which have been growing on earth since the time of the dinosaurs. The park also has some interesting features: a lake with giant fountains and various sham buildings, to which Berardo has added a collection of *azulejos*, Chinese vases and other curios. One of the vases, made in South Africa by Portuguese and Brazilian artisans. It is 5.345m (17.5ft) high (the world's tallest vase) and weighs 550kg. There is also an extraordinary Japanese Garden, about halfway down the hill between the entrance and the lake. The Portuguese have a long history in Japan and this is told in a large series of colourful azulejos designed by Alberto Cedrón, but produced in Lisbon. To add to the theme there are pagodas and Japanese plants, as well as a whole array of other curios, including several fountains.

Now walk back to the church steps and the **wicker toboggans** which all visitors should use to return to Funchal. But before taking the toboggan, a quite short (but distinctly uphill) walk or taxi ride should be taken to the **Terreiro da Luta** on the hill above the village. This was the site of the vision of the Virgin Mary to the young Monte girl and the finding of the miraculous statue. The *azulejo* representation of the story in Monte church is reproduced on the base of huge memorial and statue of the Virgin which now stands on the terrace. But the statue is not only a reminder of that miraculous find, having been erected as a result of a vow by the Madeiran people in 1916. In that year a German submarine sank several ships, including a French warship, in Funchal harbour, then surfaced and shelled the city. A similar raid was carried out in 1917. The Madeirans, fearful of further raids or invasion, vowed that if they were spared, when peace returned they would erect a statue to the Virgin in thanks. It was not until 1926 that they were able to carry out their promise. In that year the basalt pedestal and column - a total height of 5.5m (18ft) - was erected and topped with a fine statue. The rosary around the pedestal is made from the anchor chain of the sunken French warship. weighed down by large stones carried to the site by

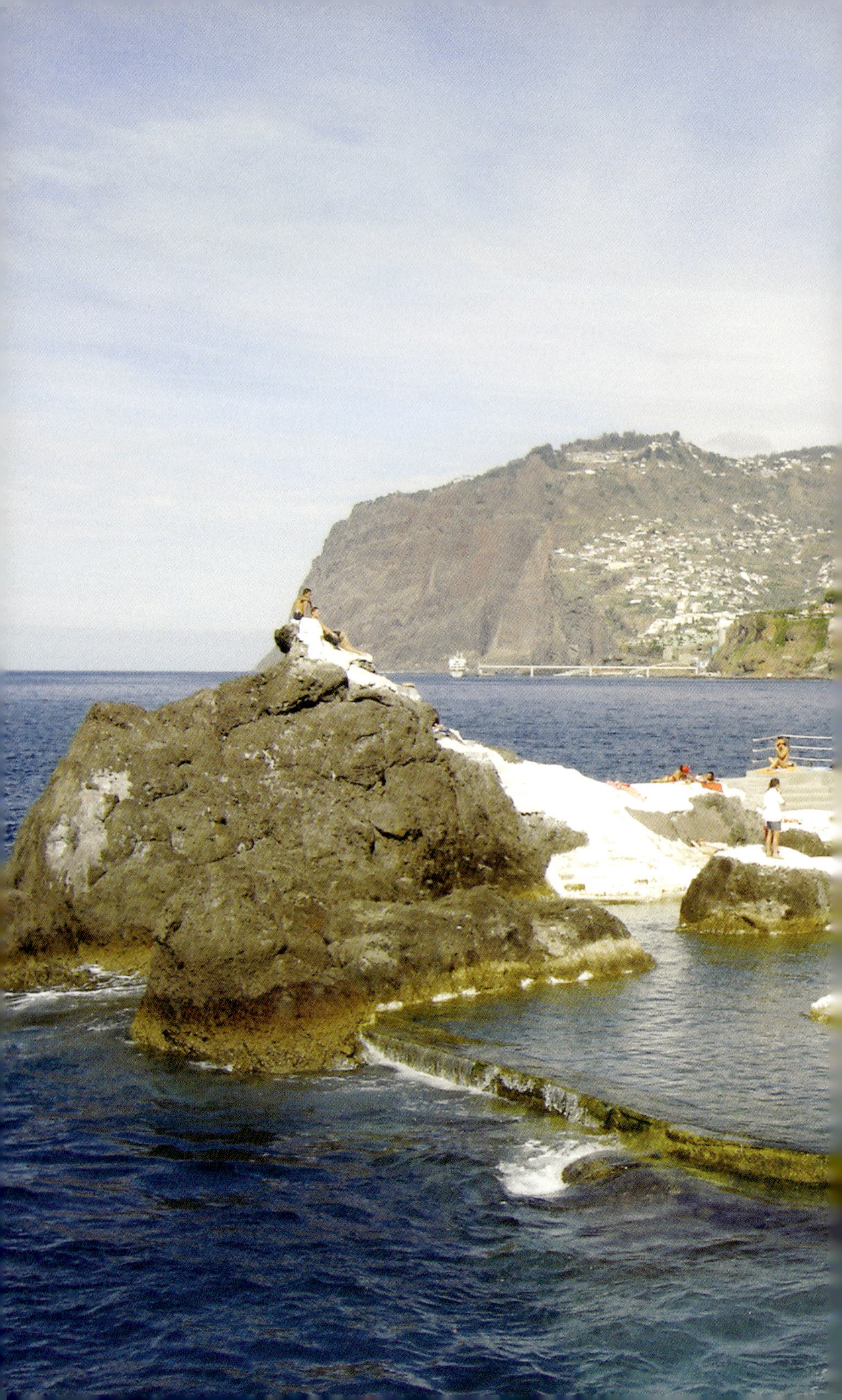

Doca do Cavacasn Swimming Pool, Funchal

faithful Madeirans.

The view from the terrace on which the memorial stands is magnificent, looking over Monte to Funchal and the coast. Close to the statue is a chapel with *pax* (peace) set above the red art deco door in its lantern-like entranceway.

The terrace was once the terminus of the funicular railway from Funchal and the old top station can still be seen. In its garden is a statue of Zarco sculpted by Francisco Franco in 1919 to celebrate the 500th anniversary of the island's discovery.

Curral das Freiras

Though further from the city centre than any of the other attractions visited so far in this chapter, a visit to Curral das Freiras is an out-and-back excursion, the track from the village which heads north cross the high peaks to Boaventura and the north coast at present only being negotiable by four-wheel drive vehicles.

To reach the village, head west through Funchal's hotel zone, then turn northwards along ER 107, soon reaching the **Pico dos Barcelos**, a well-known viewpoint of the city. There is a restaurant here, as well as a collection of souvenir seller, but the highlight is the view. The number of viewing terraces - too many for the even the most crowded tourist day - is for locals who come here to view the Funchal fireworks festival on New Year's Eve.

Beyond the viewpoint the road soon leaves the western sprawl of Funchal/São Martinho/Santo Antonio behind and begins to climb through the fragrant eucalyptus woods. At one point the road goes through a tunnel: just before reaching this, follow the obvious track on the right for the **Eira do Serrado**. There are more souvenir sellers at the car park, but that is not why you have come: take the paved path for the *miradouro*, following it through chestnut woods - the butterflies are excellent here at the right time of year - to reach the viewpoint. The view is breathtaking, arguably the best on the island, with the village of **Curral das Freiras** sat in what is often described, understandably, as a cauldron. Until fairly recently geologists though the feature was a volcanic crater, and with its almost circular enclosure of sheer basalt cliffs that is certainly how it appears: now, however, it is generally agreed that the amphitheatre is not volcanic in origin, but was created by differential erosion of the rock by the steep, fast-flowing stream in the hollow. It is though that the stream wore away softer volcanic tufa to expose the hard, resistant basalt. If that is the case then the cauldron is a wonder of natural erosion.

After taking in the view - this will take time, the sheer size of the hollow, and its depth taking several minutes to absorb - continue along the road, going through a further tunnel and then negotiating several hairpin bends to arrive, rather abruptly, in the village.

Curral das Freiras means 'the corral (or stable) of the nuns', this being the secret hollow to which the nuns of the convent of Santa Clara in Funchal fled when the French pirate Bertrand de Montluc raided the city in 1566. It is no surprise that the nuns found safety here. Until the late 1950s there was

Places to Visit

Jardim Botânico (Botanical Garden and Natural History Museum)
Quinta do Bom Successo
Caminho do Meio
Open: Garden - All year, daily 9am-6pm, Museum: All year, daily 9am-5.30pm.
☎ 211200
The Garden is reach by Horãrios do Funchal bus 31.

Jardim de Loiros (Tropical Bird Garden)
Caminho de Meio
Open: All year, daily 9am-6pm
☎ 211200

Jardim Orquídea (Orchid Garden)
Rua Pita da Silva, 37
Bom Successo
Open: All year, daily 9am-6pm.
☎ 238444
The Garden is reach by Horãrios do Funchal buses 29, 30 or 31.

Quinta do Palheiro Ferreiro (Blandy's Garden)
Palheiro Ferreiro
Open: All year, Mon-Fri 10am-12.30pm.
☎ 793044
The Garden is reach by Horãrios do Funchal buses 29, 36 or 37.

Jardim do Monte Palace (Monte Tropical Gardens)
Caminho do Monte, 174
Monte
Open: All year, Mon-Sat 9am-6pm.
☎ 782339
The Garden is reach by Horãrios do Funchal buses 20 and 21.

---

no motorable road into the hollow, all incoming and outgoing goods being carried in by mule along a track which can still be followed. (The mule track descent from Eira do Serrado - see the chapter on Walking on Madeira - is a fascinating way to reach the village.)

From the village the mountain hollow is almost as impressive a sight as it was from Eira do Serrado. The villagers have terraced the lower slopes to grow fruit and vegetables, but the most popular local crop is the chestnut which is used to make soup, flour - the chestnut cakes, especially if warm, are the perfect accompaniment to a coffee - and a liqueur of awesome potency. Cherry and walnut based liqueurs are also produced and are equally potent. At the centre of the village is a church built in the nineteenth century by Santa Clara's nuns to replace the original chapel raised by the sister three centuries earlier.

3. Western Madeira

Below: Rabaçal

This is the longest of our Madeiran tours, only a little over 160km (100 miles) in length, but the twisting south coast road followed on the return makes for a very slow drive, particularly from Achadas da Cruz to Calheta. Some visitors might consider an overnight stop in Porto Moniz, though with an early start you will be back in Funchal for dinner.

Funchal to Porto Moniz

From Funchal, follow the expressway westwards, then reverse the central island tour as far as the Boca da Encumeada. There, turn left along ER 110 (signed for Bica da Cana/Paúl da Serra) a route which climbs through wild, uninhabited country (and also climbs through the occasional tunnel), with marvellous views, to reach **Bica da Cana**, a noted viewpoint, the view being the north coast, east towards the high peaks and westward across the high plateau.

The plateau is the next objective. **Paúl da Sierra** means mountain desert and is a very apt description. It is believed that the plateau began life as relatively flat layer of lava, this weathering into a thin volcanic soil which, together with the permeable rock beneath it and the wind which often scours the plateau, keeps the vegetation to a minimum. On the plateau, the lush, colourful vegetation visitors have come to know on other Madeiran tours is a memory, though in spring and summer there is the occasional burst of yellow from flowering broom bushes. But strangely the plateau is as important to the creation of the 'other' Madeiran as any single feature, the permeable rock sucking up water like a giant sponge. The water percolates down through the rock until it reaches a layer of impermeable clay. It then emerges from the ground as a series of springs and waterfalls whose flow is captured by the rivers which create the lush valleys, and by the *levadas* which irrigate the coastal lands. Surface water - rain and odd pools where the rock is less permeable - is also taken from the plateau in *levadas*.

Despite the relative lack of vegetation the plateau supports sheep and goats, and the occasional cow, too, the lack of steep drops and terracing meaning these lucky cows are the only ones on the island which are allowed to roam freely. The sheep and goats are semi-wild, seeing a shepherd only during an annual round up in the summer. Anciently the shepherds shared the plateau with their flocks, and visitors who take time to explore may find the shelters the men used as a protection against the wind and cold. The more modern structures on the plateau - they are more easily spotted too - are the wind turbines. More are to be added, making Paúl de Serra one of Madeira's most important sources of electricity.

Ignore the turning to the left, a difficult road which plunges down a series of hairpin bends to reach Canhas, and then, soon after, one on the right which crosses the bleak landscape of Fanal to reach Porto Moniz. The road now drops off the plateau and soon reaches a turn, on the right, for **Rabaçal**. The road descends steeply, is single track (with limited passing places) and blind corners: please go slowly, use your horn and listen for another horn. The road also crosses a river - the Ribeira do Alecrim (*alecrim* means rosemary, the herb growing on its banks) - before reaching a 'car park' and government resthouse. It is only 2km (1.25 miles) from the main road (though it can feel a lot further). There is nothing at Rabaçal apart from the resthouse - reserved for government officials - but the spot is as good as its name, rabaçal meaning unspoilt, and is the start point for a couple of magnificent walks, one of which - to the Risco waterfall - should be on the itinerary of even committed non-walkers. The path is straightforward, passing beneath trees who branches overhang the walker like the grasping hands in some gothic fairy tale, and it takes only about 20 minutes to reach the falls. They are about 100m (over 300ft) high. For the very best view, go under the falls - there is a tunnel, but you are still likely to get damp - emerging to a fine viewpoint. Full details of this walk and another from Rabaçal are given in the chapter on Walking in Madeira.

Beyond the turn to Rabaçal there are several more fine viewpoints, both of the local high land and of the coast.

Then the road starts to descend. Almost at once the vegetation changes, firstly to heather and then to laurel forest. At a road junction a turn right leads to Santa and then down a hairpinned road to Porto Moniz (both on the Central Island tour), but we turn left towards Madeira's western tip.

Porto Moniz to Calheta

The section of road from the turning to Calheta is the most unspoilt on the island. Few visitors come this far and you will find the locals as interested in you as you are in them. Go past the village of Achadas da Cruz and continue along a difficult, twisting road to reach **Ponta do Pargo**, a village named for the headland to the west. That headland, named for the dolphins which were once frequently seen off-shore, is the actual western tip of Madeira. There is a lighthouse at the tip, a white building with an elegant red cap. The lighthouse is now automatic, but it is said that the last keeper still lives in it because he could not bear to leave. If you look west from the headland there is only sea, thousands of miles of it, as the next land is the coast of South Carolina. The village is a quiet, relaxed place - unless you come in September when the apple fair is a time for celebration with music and dancing, and a great deal of noise.

Soon after leaving Ponta do Pargo the road turns east - you are now heading back towards Funchal, though it will be sometime before you arrive: it is only about 22km (14 miles) from Ponta do Pargo to Calheta, but is could easily take you an hour to get there. The scenery the road passes through changes now, becoming more pastoral with more grass and flowers, and more trees. The character of the road itself does not change though, as it twists its way eastwards. A road off to the right threads a seemingly uneasy way between outcrops of red rock to reach **Paúl do Mar** a village that until recently was reached only by sea. There is a harbour with the usual colourful boats bobbing gently, a massive sea wall, a huddle of houses and groups of villagers who will eye you curiously.

Most visitors will ignore Paúl do Mar, but may be more tempted by **Jardim do Mar**, the 'garden by the sea' seeming a more welcoming spot than the 'desert by the sea'. The drive to this village is awkward, too, - a new road is being built between Paúl do Mar and Jardim do Mar which may improve the situation - but it certainly has a garden feel, with bougainvillaea, passion flowers and other colourful blooms, and patches of exotic fruit trees - avocado and papaya. The turn for Jardim do Mar is reached just beyond **Prazeres** where a new hotel (the Jardim Atlântico) suggests that this section of the coast may soon be developed. The view from the new hotel is a fine advert for Madeira.

The view ahead improves as **Estreito da Calheta** is reached. The village is worth a stop to see the lovely Capela dos Reis Magos - the chapel of the Three Magi (the Three Kings) - at the western end. The chapel is sixteenth century and has some good Manueline carvings and a wooden ceiling in Mujedar style. There is also a sixteenth century depiction of the Magi on the altar. Beyond the village, continue into Calheta.

Calheta to Ponta do Sol

Calheta was once the main centre of Madeira's sugar industry and the disused chimneys of several sugar mills can still be seen. One mill still operates producing *aguardente*, the Madeiran rum, and some molasses. In the days of the sugar industry all sugar coming into Calheta was taxed, the money collected making the village a very prosperous place. Today the local prosperity - much reduced from those old days - is based on wine and cereals. Calheta is another of Madeira's very ancient settlements, in this case having the proof of a charter dated 1502, rather than oral tradition and later reference. The church is older than the charter, probably dating from the 1430s, though it was substantially rebuilt in the seventeenth century. Inside, it has a fine wooden ceiling in Mujedar style and a tabernacle of ebony inlaid with silver.

The road now runs close to the sea, with fine views of the ridges of the high inland peaks as they finally fall into the sea. Just before a pair of tunnels which lead to Madalena do Mar, a narrow road leads inland, going uphill to several fine viewpoints and the villages of **Arco da Calheta**, where the church - on the village's western edge - has another fine wooden ceiling. It is claimed that the chapel was the benefaction of a daughter-in-law of João Gonçalves Zarco. Further on is **Canhas** which, on the first Sunday of each month, is the scene of an important religious

Western Madeira

Paul do Mar

procession with folk from all over the island following a Via Sacra past the Stations of the Cross to a huge Crucifix, a monument to St Teresa. The procession is followed by an open-air mass. From the two villages a narrow, winding and unforgiving road heads uphill to reach the main road across the Paúl da Serra.

Madalena do Mar, the next village on the coast road, was, in the fifteenth century, the home of Henry the German.

The church is said to have been founded by Henrique, and one version of his story claims that his body was washed ashore, retrieved and buried within it. The house where Henrique lived is close to the church, distinguishable by the curious coat-of-arms.

Ponta do Sol to Ribeira Brava

Beyond Madalena the road continues in fine style, hugging the shore line and diving into a couple of tunnels before reaching **Ponta do Sol**, a village named for the rounded headland it occupies and for the sun. Madeira's south coast is the sunniest part of island, and the headland is one of the few places which sees the sun throughout the day, most of the other south coast villages being, at some time, shadowed by cliffs or hills. Because of the sun it receives the village is Madeira's major producer of bananas, the hillsides being terraced and every available piece of flat land being planted with the fruit. The growers claim that the rock faces act as a storage radiator, being warmed by the sun during the day, then keeping the bananas warm at night, and that this helps them ripen a little earlier than at other places on the island, helping the Ponta growers export their crop sooner which, in turn, earns a slightly higher price for the fruit. That the Ponta bananas ripen first is undeniable, but the idea that this is due to a rock face radiator rather than the extra hours of sun the village receives seems extremely unlikely. The village also has one of the island's main packing plants for bananas, though the packed fruit is taken by lorry to Funchal for shipment as the nineteenth century harbour is not big enough for container ships. The big piles of plant residue beside the packing plant is eventually processed into animal feedstuff.

Praia Seixal

Ponta do Sol's harbour is a favourite stopping place with tourist coaches, and this is no surprise, with its neat row of houses, stubby palm trees and magnificently eccentric coffee kiosk it is well worth a walk. From the harbour a cobbled street leads to the church which has some fine azulejos, a superb wooden Mujedar ceiling and a green ceramic font which is believed to have been a gift from King Manuel I.

Ponta do Sol to Funchal

On the road inland from Ponta do Sol there are several good viewpoints of the village, before the hamlet of **Lombada** is reached. Here a *quinta* built by João Esmeraldo is now used as a school. Esmeraldo was a friend of Christopher Columbus and owned a local sugar plantation. It is said that Columbus visited the mansion several times.

Back on the coast, the road maintains its shore-hugging and tunnelling style to reach **Ribeira Brava**, a village named for the 'wild river' on whose mouth it sits. The village is a lovely place, quietly elegant and very welcoming, with plenty of choice for a coffee. The number of coffee shops is a reminder of the village's old importance - folk crossing the Encumeada Pass, or following the south coast towards Funchal met here and the village acquired a reputation as a meeting place for old friends and as a place where business deals could be struck.

The village's main square is paved in basalt and marble and planted with scented trees. Facing it is the church, dedicated to São Bento (St Benedict), a neat, simple building with a bell tower whose clock faces and *azulejo*-faced final pyramid belie that description. Inside there is an unusual stone font, another which is said to have been a present from King Manuel I. The font is carved with fruit and animals, some of which are picked out in paint. There are similar carvings on the pulpit, and a painting of the day in 1848 when the statue of Our Lady of Fatima spent a day in the church on its tour of the Catholic world.

Behind the church is the Town Hall, a recently restored merchant's house bearing the date 1776. The house's garden has also been restored and is now open as a small public park. From the Town Hall, walk away from the sea to reach the Madeiran Ethnography Museum with a collection which explores the fascinating culture of the island, with sections on crafts and

Ponta da Sol and John Dos Passos

Lovers of the work of the American writer John Dos Passos (the author of Manhattan Transfer among other works) who died in 1970 may be interested in the plaque in Rua Principe Dom Luis I. Dos Passos' grandfather was born in Ponta, emigrating with his family to Chicago in the mid-nineteenth century. John Dos Passos, who was born in 1896, visited the village several times, the plaque recording his last visit in 1960.

Henrique Alemão - Henry the German

Henrique was so called because the locals could not understand the guttural language he spoke. Historians now think that he was actually King Wladislaw III of Poland whose army was, in 1444, crushed by an Otteman army. The King was said to have been killed in the battle, but it is believed that shame at the disastrous showing of his army and at the way he had let his country down meant he faked his death and resolved to go on a pilgrimage to the Holy Land to atone. There is evidence that the king completed the pilgrimage, but he then disappears from history. It is believed that he crossed Europe to Portugal and there was given land on Madeira by the king. It is certainly the case that Henrique, the curious foreigner, held a large estate at Madalena, and that be often sailed to Funchal to speak with João Gonçalves Zarco.

At Madalena Henrique married a local girl - language seemingly no problem to the union - and that they had a son called Sigismundo. Then, during another trip to see Zarco, Henrique is said to have been recognised by two Polish monks, though quite what they might have been doing on Madeira is not explained. The story now takes on a mythical feel, though elements of it are clearly factual. Henrique told Zarco the monks were not only mistaken but malevolent and they were sent back to Portugal. Soon after, a message came from Lisbon that Henrique was to return to the mainland - had the monks retold their story in Lisbon and frightened the Portuguese court? Henrique set sail, but his ship was wrecked and he was drowned. The distraught Sigismundo, who had never been told the truth of his father's origins, was determined to sail to Portugal to find out why Henrique had been summoned. His ship too foundered and the lad was drowned. With the deaths there was no requirement for anyone at the Portuguese court to explain, and it is left to the historian to ponder on the true identify of Henrique the German.

costume. Elsewhere, the village's narrow cobbled streets are worth exploring, as is the sea front, this leading to the harbour: Ribeira Brava began life as fishing port and the nearby open market still sells the daily catch as well as fruit and vegetables. Close to where the wild river reaches the sea stand the remains of a seventeenth century fortress, built to ward off pirate attacks. At the end of June the fort is the start point for the procession which begins the Festa de São Pedro, a festival which includes day-long folk music and dancing exhibitions.

From the village the road follows the river, but soon reaches the new expressway which is followed back to Funchal.

Place to Visit

Ethnography Museum
Rua de São Francisco
Ribeira Brava
Open: All year, Tuesday-Sunday
10am-12.30pm, 2-6pm
☎ 952598

4. Central Madeira

Opposite: Porto Moniz

This fine tour crosses the high mountains of central Madeira twice, once by way of the Paso de Poiso to reach Faial and the north coast, and again on a return from São Vicente over the Encumeada pass. It is a long tour - not far in terms of the kilometres covered, but taking a long time because of twisting nature of the mountain and north coast roads. Start early and enjoy the sun rising on the first mountain pass and going down on the second.

Funchal to Faial

From Funchal take the road (ER 102) to Monte, continuing past the village and the Terreiro do Luta. To this point the road has been flanked by acacia and eucalyptus trees, but as you climb these are replaced by laurel and pine and the occasional Madeiran cedar, now a sadly rare tree. The laurels are *Laurus azorica* and *Appolonius barbujana* (Canary Island laurel), but much of the pine has been planted recently in an attempt to recreate the original island forest. Maritime pine is one of the new trees, a reasonable choice, but others include Douglas fir and Lawson cypress which seem somewhat dubious selections. Soon the crossroads near the is reached. The pass is at a height of 1,400m (4,592ft) and is actually more of a saddle point (or col).

Pico de Arieiro

At the pass, turn left for a short detour to the summit of Pico de Arieiro at 1,818m (5,963ft) Madeira's third highest peak. As it rises the road leaves the laurel and, finally, the pine forest behind, climbing through heather and weatherswept grass by the time the top is reached. Little climbing is required to tick off this notable summit, the road actually reaching to within a few metres of the top. It finishes by a *pousada* (guesthouse) which has a good restaurant and a small bar. The guesthouse was built in the 1980s, almost two centuries after the other, apparently insignificant, building passed just before reaching the top. This was an ice house, winter's snow being compressed into slabs of ice which were then stored for summer shipment to the hotels and mansions of the rich in Funchal.

As might be expected, the view from the peak is remarkable - but there is a snag. Often the clouds form around the peak by late morning or lunchtime, blocking out any hope of a view. It is possible for the clouds to sink below the peak, and if that is the case then the view is enhanced, the high peaks poking through a sea of cloud. There is, of course, no way to guarantee clear weather - though the local weather forecast can help - but to stand the best chance come very, very early, perhaps arriving with the dawn. The guesthouse was built because so many people wanted to stay at the summit to catch the early morning view. Those folk also maintain that the night sky from Pico do Arieiro is amazing, the lack of local lights and the clarity of the air making it as good as at the best observatories.

If your conditions are good, with clear skies and the promise of nothing but sunshine, you should consider the walk to Pico Ruivo, Madeira's highest peak (at 1,862m - 6,107ft) takes about 2 hours each way. If you intend to try it, please be sure you have warm clothing - it can be very cold on the tops if the sun disappears. It is also advisable to take waterproofs and even some food and drink - there is a café below the summit of Pico Ruivo and the bar and guesthouse here, but at half distance between the two it can seem like a long way both ahead and behind. There is a paved path almost all of the way between the peaks, so it is difficult to get lost. The exposed sections of this path are fitted with guide rails, but anyone with a dread of heights is advised to settle for the view from Pico do Arieiro. Finally, the section of path at about half distance is prone to landslides: if it looks as though there has been a slide - if the guide rails and path have disappeared, please turn back. For full details of the walk, see the chapter on Walking in Madeira p.122.

Continuing to Faial

Return to Paso de Poiso and turn left for Faial and the north coast. The road descends through a section of original laurel forest, now a Parque Forestal, set up to preserve this increasingly rare natural habitat. At **Ribeiro Frio** there is a short nature trail through the forest, worth taking to see the Pride of Madeira with its dense blue flowers, the yellow Madeiran foxgloves and even orchids. The village - really little more than a hamlet of scattered farms and a restaurant, a favourite stopping place for tour coaches - is named for the 'cold river' which flows down from the high peaks. The oxygen-rich water of the stream is used in the island's only trout hatchery and farm, the fish being raised to stock rivers throughout the island (in part to develop fishing as a tourist/leisure activity) and also to stock the tables of island restaurants. The hatchery is open to visitors - no charge, access at any reasonable time - and the fish are, of course, on the menu of the restaurant. From Ribeiro Frio one of the island's easier *levada* walks leads to the excellent viewpoint of Balçoes: take the signed path to the left just below the shop, following the dry *levada*, then forking right where the *levada* goes left to reach the viewpoint.

As the road drops from the village it emerges from the forest to an intensely cultivated area, with *poios* (terraces) climbing the hillside. Be careful here as you will likely pass local folk struggling under the weight of overloaded conical baskets. After a particularly winding section of road there is a choice of routes, the main road bending back on itself, while a right turn follows a road which heads straight for the cube-shaped Penha de Águia (Eagle's Rock - see the Eastern Island tour). Both roads descend quickly to reach Faial, passing through an area of fruit orchards - mangoes, papaya and passion fruit, with occasional small plantations of bananas in sheltered spots - and cattle farms. In the cattle fields you will often see palheiros, the typical A-shaped byres of wood and thatch for which Santana (visited later on the tour) is famous.

Faial is named for the wax myrtle tree (called faia in Portuguese) a native plant of the Azores and Madeira which grew in abundance locally when the first settlers arrived. Clearance of the hillside for terrace farming has now made it a rarity, though it is still possible to find specimens. With its waxy, aromatic leaf it is quite distinctive. From the village square, with its neat eighteenth century church (the belltower is particularly attractive), there is a good view of the coast and of Eagle Rock. Despite the name there are no eagles here, though the osprey - a very rare Madeiran bird - does nest.

Santana

Drive through Faial, admiring the pretty, but scattered, houses which make up this pleasant village (the houses are an indication of the relative prosperity of the area, the land here being very fertile) and continue to **Santana**. The village is named for the mother of the Virgin Mary and is one of the most picturesque on Madeira, with its collection of *palheiro* houses and the other pretty cottages. As with nearby Faial, Santana's neatness derives from the fertility of the local soil which supports not only dozens of fruit orchards - soft fruit and kiwi as well as the more conventional fruit trees (figs, plums, cherries and apples) - but vegetables, potatoes and cereals. The village is the scene of one of Madeira's most curious festivals, the Festa do Campadres (literally the Festival of Married Couples) in February as part of the Madeiran carnival season. A husband and wife, life-size figures of straw are placed before a 'court' of villagers. After a case for prosecution and defence which are little more then hilarious attacks on government policy and official figures, a decision is reached and both the figures are burnt. There is then a more conventional carnival with music and dancing.

From Santana two roads head south towards the high peak. The first, at the edge of the town first reached, climbs up to **Achada do Teixeira**. Here the road ends, but a paved path continues to the top of Pico Ruivo. Achada do Teixeira is at 1,590m (5,215ft), the 2km (1.25 mile), 272m (892ft) climb to Madeira's highest peak taking about an hour (see chapter on Walking in Madeira). Just below the summit there is a café/rest house. The ascent is worthwhile not only because Pico Ruivo is Madeira's highest peak, but because the summit often pokes above the cloud which swirls around the high mountains. If that is the case the walk up can be uninspiring, but the view across on ocean of cloud is tremendous. Of course, it is an even better view in clear weather.

The second road heading south leaves close to the centre of Santana, going uphill to **Queimadas**, where the cluster of thatched houses are mountain retreats reserved for officials of the

Madeiran government. The authorities could hardly have chosen a more idyllic place for themselves, the local area being rich in azaleas and rhododendrons, as well as a profusion of native flowers. Queimadas is the start point for a magnificent walk (see chapter on Walking on Madeira p.122).

Santana to São Vicente

Beyond Santana the north coast road twists around the gorge of the Ribeiro **São Jorge** before reaching the village for which the river is named. São Jorge is another prosperous village, often ignored by the tourist coaches that stop at As Cabanas (a tourist complex further along the road where local produce and crafts are sold). That is a pity because the main square has a park with lovely azaleas and Bird of Paradise flowers, and the church is well worth visiting.

The church is eighteenth century, built to replace one which was destroyed by floods. It is in lavish Baroque style, with several intricately carved altars decorated with gold leaf. Some of the gold leaf is missing or peeling, but enough remains for the splendour of the original work to be appreciated. The main altar has scenes from the life of St George (for whom the village is named). The church also has some excellent *azulejos*. The village sits on a ridge of rock which pushes out towards the sea. On a high point of the ridge there is a lighthouse from which the view along the coast is superb.

Continue along the road as it snakes its way to **Arco de São Jorge**, a neat little village. From the As Cabanas tourist complex there is an excellent view of the village, which is named for the arch of mountain to the south. A tunnel pierces the western edge of the arch, taking the road into the gorge of the Ribeiro do Ponco. From the head of the gorge, in Fajã do Penedo, a road heads south into the mountains. This is the line of an old track which crosses the high peaks to reach Curral das Freiras.

On the far side of the gorge the road passes several picturesque waterfalls before arriving in **Boaventura**, a tiny hamlet renowned for the growing of the white willow canes used in Camacha's wickerwork industry. Beyond the village the road reaches the coast, following it closely before diving into a tunnel from which it exits into **Ponte Delgada**. When the church was being built here, in the late fifteenth century, a Crucifix was washed ashore. The villagers saw this as a sign from heaven and the Crucifix was venerated for centuries. Sadly in 1908 the church was destroyed by fire. The crucifix was badly burnt, but the charred remains were rescued, placed in a glass case and remain the object of pilgrimages. Each year, on the first Sunday in September, a festival is held in honour of the Crucifix, the village and the church being covered in flowers. It is claimed that the festival is the oldest on Madeira: it is certainly one of the most colourful. The village also has an interesting swimming pool, close to the church. The pool is tidal, its Atlantic waters cleaned and refilled by each new tide.

Beyond Ponte Delgada the road hugs the coast, taking a line along a terrace - part natural, part carved - and one

Central Madeira

Faial

São Vicente

requiring the assistance of a tunnel to make progress between cliffs and the sea. So close are the cliffs to the left that occasionally a waterfall offers it services as an impromptu car wash. This section of road is one of the most impressive on the island, and it is almost with regret that the inland turn to São Vicente is reached.

A Detour to Seixal and Porto Moniz

The exuberance of the coastal road can continue to be enjoyed by taking a detour from the São Vicente turn to Porto Moniz. For those wanting to explore the whole island, the section of coast from São Vicente to Porto Moniz is a nuisance - take a detour as part of this tour and the north cost road must be reversed (though in view of its wild attractions that is hardly a drawback). The detour to Porto Moniz from the western island tour is easy enough, but that leaves the coastal road past Seixal unseen. On balance it is better to detour from here.

From the road junction, continue along ER 101, passing the gold and souvenir shop on the left, then following a road that was hewn from solid rock by pickaxe and shovel at a rate of about 1km per year, a monument to physical effort and perseverance in the days before mechanical excavators made such tasks seem commonplace. Please be cautious: the road is often single track with passing places and the drop to the sea is occasionally poorly protected and extremely unforgiving. The road executes one delightful sweeping semi-circular curve around

a sharp chasm, then disappears into a tunnel before reaching a wonderful view of tiny offshore islands, the jagged coast near Seixal and the gorge of the Ribeiro do Inferno (named by the road builders?). **Seixal** is renowned for its vine terraces which grow the grapes for Sercial wine. To protect the vines from the blast of the Atlantic winds - Seixal being set on an exposed rib of mountain - the villagers have planted hedges, reinforcing them with bracken and heather. Seixal is also a fishing port with a collection of colourful boats: it seems a perilously exposed place to earn such a living. From close to the village a difficult road heads inland along the valley of the Seixal river, a picturesque valley with some dramatic scenery.

Beyond Seixal, where there is a excellent coffee shop, the coast road continues in similarly dramatic fashion the highlight being a viewpoint, just before Porto Moniz is reached, of the famous off-shore rock through which the elements have carved a window. The window (*janela* in Portuguese) has given its name to the river which reaches the sea here - the **Ribeira da Janela** - to the off-shore islands clustered around the windowed rock - the Ilhéus da Ribeira da Janela - and even to the village perched above the river (which shares the river's name - Ribeira da Janela). The village is the site of several hydro-electric power stations, utilising the fast-flowing locals streams to generate electricity. Heading south from Ribeira da Janela is a track - passable with a four-wheel drive vehicle piloted by an enthusiastic driver - which leads up into the mountains, reach ER 110 on Paul da Serra. The track crosses one of the wildest, most remote areas of the island. Though lower than the high peaks to the east, the country seems more desolate - there are a few trees (while there are none on the Picos), but their bent, stunted forms seems merely to add to the bleak feel of the place. Yet the area has a strange attraction, its very harshness being picturesque. It is a marvellous walking area, with occasional impressive long views - but be cautious, it the clouds come down and you are off the road it can be difficult to find, and this is no place to be lost. For a short walk on the edge of this fine country see the chapter on Walking in Madeira (p.122).

Porto Moniz is named for Francisco Moniz, a minor nobleman from the Algarve who married one of João Gonçalves Zarco's grand-daughters and settled at this extreme north-western tip of the island. For centuries the village was a fishing port, remote from the rest of the island, which could only be reached by boat. But now, despite the distance from the airport, Porto Moniz is undergoing something of a tourist boom. It is the site of Madeira's only official camp sites, a fact which attracts many islanders (and a few visitors on low budgets), but also has several new hotels. One side effect is that most of the old fishermen's cottages close to the harbour are being demolished and their sites re-developed: visit now while a little of the old fishing village remains intact. At the harbour the remains of a castle built in the seventeenth century to defend the village from pirate attack can also be seen.

The harbour is protected by a finger of rock extending towards the island of Ilhéu Mole (which also helps protect the harbour), making Porto Moniz the safest port on the northern coast. This probably attracted the pirates the castle was built to repel, but later encouraged some of Madeira's whaling fleet to abandon Caniçal in Porto Moniz's favour.

Close to the harbour - by the Calhau restaurant - the sea has carved a number of rock pools in the volcanic rock and these have been cleverly deepened and linked by channels and paths to create natural pools in which visitors and locals can lounge luxuriously and watch the sea. The pools are replenished each high tide, but are sufficiently small for the sun to warm then quickly. Just a few bubbles short of a jacuzzi (which sounds like an insult, but isn't!) they are a delight, worth all of the very moderate entrance fee.

A walk is worthwhile in Porto Moniz, passing quaint houses and fields whose crops (including vines) are protected (as at Seixal) by short windbreaks of bracken and heather. In the central square is the village church, a fine seventeenth century building and a couple of shops which reinforce the image of a developing tourist centre. One shop actually sells bucket and spades which seems a little optimistic as Porto Moniz is just about as far as it is possible to get from Madeira's only sandy beach.

From Porto Moniz, ER 101 climbs a series of hairpin bends which allow a wonderful view of the village. The road then climbs in a more relaxed fashion, passing through the hamlet of **Santa**. To the north-west of the hamlet is Ponta do Tristão. When Madeira was divided into fiefdoms controlled by

João Gonçalves Zarco and Tristão Vaz Teixeira the line of division was drawn from Ponta do Tristão to Ponta do Oliveira, to the east of Funchal, near Caniço. Given the difficulties of surveying such a line it seems an extraordinary choice. Apparently when Porto Moniz was first settled it was called Porto Tristão, but the name was changed as it was occasionally confused with Ponta do Tristão, a confusion which reduced Teixeira's holding.

São Vicente to Encumeada

But we are not taking ER 101, returning along the magnificent north coast road and bearing right on ER 104 to reach **São Vicente**.

São Vicente is a beautifully positioned, wonderfully picturesque, village, worthy of an exploration just for its neatness and the constant backdrop of green slopes and jagged skylines. The church is seventeenth century: inside there is some fine Baroque carving and a wealth of *azulejos*, some decorated with religious scenes, but some showing scenes from Madeiran country life. To the south of the village centre there is also a more modern church, consisting simply of a prominent bell tower. Built in the 1940s and dedicated to Our Lady of Fatima, the church/bell tower seems little used despite its newness. Also just outside the village are the Grutas de São Vicente. Unlike normal showcaves produced by the erosion of passages and creation of stalagmites and stalactites by water, these caves were produced by lava flows from the Paúl de Serra. Occasionally flowing lava can cool on top and bottom to such an extent that it solidifies, forming a rock tube through which molten lave continues to flow. If the flow empties the tube then it remains as a hollow lava tube. That is what has happened here at São Vicente and visitors can explore the lava tubes, a fascinating journey.

The belltower is passed on the journey along ER 104 which follows the valley of the Ribeiro de São Vicente before climbing steeply uphill. At a tight 180° bend there is a marvellous view back down the valley to the village.

Beyond, the road becomes even steeper, climbing to the **Boca do Encumeada**, the Encumeada Pass at 1,007m (3,302ft). The pass offers what is arguably the most interesting view on the island. If it is clear the view northwards is of the São Vicente Valley and the sea, while to the south is the Ribeira Brava valley and the sea, the pass being one of the few places where the northern and southern coasts can both be seen. To add to the interest, to the east are Madeira's highest peaks, while to the west the land rises towards the high plateau of Paúl da Serra. After enjoying the view you can enjoy a drink, or even a meal, in the fine restaurant of the Residencial Encumeada, the excellent hotel just below the top.

Encumeada to Funchal

From the pass, take ER 104 which heads towards the south coast, soon reaching another viewpoint (below the Fajã des Éguas). In the foreground of the view is the village of **Serra de Água**. The village is bypassed by the

Palheiros

Below: Casas de Santana

The country around Santana is the best area to see palheiros, the typical Madeiran A-shaped building, most often seen as a cowshed, but still used for housing in the town. The use of a wooden A-frame and thatch from the ridge pole to the floor has two advantages - it is easy to construct and the thatch acts as a good insulator, the fact that it completely envelopes the building meaning it stays warm in winter, but cool in summer.

Originally the palheiros were used for both domestic buildings and as cow sheds. The cows were kept in the sheds for long periods - they still are on many farms - the steepness of the ground meaning they could easily injure themselves, or damage the fragile terracing if left to roam freely. The cows were fed regularly, and every few days were walked on a lead for exercise. Even today it is possible to see farmers staggering under the weight of vast bundles of hay on their way to feed their animals, and also to see tethered cows, though such sights are becoming rarer, as is the use of palheiros. Many of those that remain have lost their thatch in favour of corrugated iron - harder wearing and requiring less skilled maintenance, but much less picturesque and distinctly less romantic.

Rarer still is the use of palheiros as domestic buildings. For housing the basic design was maintained, but a floor was added in the gable, this upper storey being reached through an external door reached by a ladder: there were never internal stairs. The upper storey was for sleeping and the placing and climbing of the ladder in winter or in pouring rain must have been a trial.

Today Santana is almost the only place on the island where palheiros are still used as houses, their fronts painted in bright colours and made even more colourful by pot plants. Two houses - beyond the O Colmo restaurant (a palheiro which is used as a house is known as a Casa de Colmo) - are open to visitors and are on the itinerary of most tourist coaches. There is a third palheiro housing the public toilets! There are other, real, houses in the village where the coach-borne visitors rarely venture, the showhouses being on the road which bypasses the main village street.

main road which executes a couple of sharp bends around it. It is a pleasant little place, rather better than might be expected from its claim to fame as being the site of Madeira's first hydro-electric power station.

Below Serra de Agua the road is almost straight (itself something of an interesting sight), following the Ribeira Brava, literally the 'wild river'. In summer the volume of water emphatically belies the name, but in winter the river can indeed be a furious torrent. As the coast is approached - about 2km (1.25 miles) from the village of Ribeira Brava - you can bear left to follow the new expressway for a quick return to Funchal. To visit all the interesting places on the way it is really necessary to continue to Ribeira Brava, and then to take the winding road eastwards to reach Campanário and Quinta Grande. From the latter village the famous cliffs of Cabo Girão can be reached, one of the most photographed spots on the island. The name means the 'Cape of Turning', the turning in question being that of João Gonçalves Zarco who sailed this far before deciding he had seen enough and turned around to land at the more hospitable bay to the east (where he then founded Funchal). Gazing over the cliff from the security of the railing-ed viewpoint, the visitor could be forgiven for thinking the name might have something to do with the awesome, dizzying drop. Cabo Girão claims to be the second highest sea cliff in Europe, measuring 580m (1,900ft). As there are conflicting claims for which are the highest - are they in Norway, or, perhaps, in Iceland? - and even a debate about whether Madeira (or Iceland for that matter!) is part of Europe the cliffs position in the table of highest seems a little academic. What is certain is that they are phenomenally tall.

To the east of the cliffs is the coastal village of **Câmara de Lobos**,. The name means wolf's gorge, the wolf being the monk seal which to the Portuguese was a *lobo do mar*, a wolf of the sea, the generic name given to seals and sea-lions. When Madeira was first settled the seals were relatively common and bred in the bay: today they are one of the world's rarest sea mammals with just a few breeding on the Desertas islands.

Câmara de Lobos is, and has always been, a fishing port and has a picturesque harbour full of boats in bright primary colours. The scene delighted Sir Winston Churchill who came here often to paint it: a plaque marks the spot where he would set up his easel. But the undoubted qualities of the view mask the fact that Câmara's fishermen - who fish at night for the *espada* - and their families are among the poorest folk on the island (and the cruel butt of some distinctly unChristian comments from better-off Madeirans). The increase in the Madeiran tourist trade, and the closeness of Câmara to Funchal, means that the visitor is likely to be approached by beggars.

Near the harbour, where boats are still made in the traditional way on wooden frames, is a little fisherman's chapel built in the early 1420s (making it one of the earliest on the island) but remodelled later. Inside there are paintings depicting scenes from the life of São Pedro Telmo, the patron saint of Portuguese fishermen. There is also a Baroque altar and a delightful painted ceiling. In the main square is the sixteenth century village church, dedicated to St Sebastian, whose martyrdom is depicted inside. Like the fishermen's chapel, the church was restored in the Baroque period and has some lovely gilded wood. There are also some good *azulejos*.

Heading north-eastwards from the harbour the hilltop named the Pico da Torre, though only 200m (660ft) high, is an excellent viewpoint of the village. Continuing in the same direction reaches **Estreito da Câmara de Lobos**, a hill village with a fine nineteenth century church. The village is often called the wine capital of Madeira for the sheer number of local vineyards. In September the annual grape harvest is accompanied by one of Madeira's liveliest festivals. Realising the tourist potential of the festival - and with Funchal so close - the village has expanded the activities. The old method of pressing grapes in a large tank (called a *lagar*) in which the grapes were trodden by feet to the accompaniment of music - the time-honoured method - was re-established and visitors were invited to join in. (Of course most grapes are still pressed by machine - but that is a mere detail). Local wines are also available for testing. The islanders do not have the time to wait for this year's grape harvest to be converted into Madeiran wine, and some grape juice is fermented in the 'normal' way - unheated, unfortified, just as wine is produced on mainland Europe. This wine is usually ready for drinking in November - but there is last year's to

A Protective Chapel

Close to the road junction there is a curious chapel built into the side of a natural rock, the rock topped by a cross. Legend has it that the chapel was built in the seventeenth century, perhaps in an effort to gain protection from flooding for the village.

finish first. Many of Madeira's wine villages produce a conventional wine, usually for drinking by the locals and Madeirans who are 'in the know'. But if you ask you can try it - and at Estreito during the month-long September festival it is not necessary to ask more than once. The local wine is called *canina* and is usually described as fruity. If your trip does not coincide with the September festival, try the village's Sunday market, one of the island's more colourful weekly occasions.

From Estreito it is just a short distance to Funchal.

Places to Visit

Trout Hatchery
Ribeiro Frio
Open: Any reasonable time

Grutas e Centro do Volcanismo de São Vicente
Sítio de Pé do Paso
São Vicente
Open: All year, daily 9am-9pm (7pm from October to April)
☎ 842404

5. The Eastern Island

Opposite: Prainha Caniçal

This first tour explores the eastern end of the island, the part closest to Funchal. Though relatively short, in terms of distance covered, it visits a number of interesting sites which, together with the difficult nature of Madeiran roads - the new expressway which will make the journey to the airport, Santa Cruz and Machico shorter and easier will not be opened until 2000 - means that a whole day should be set aside, particularly if the suggested detours are followed.

Funchal to Santa Cruz

From Funchal take ER 204, heading east towards Caniço. The road starts in great style, offering tantalising glimpses of the coast before reaching **Garajau**, named by its original settlers for the terns (*garajau* means term in Portuguese) which still nest on the nearby coast. Then, and for centuries after, Garajau was a small fishing port, but it has now been almost completely taken over by the tourist trade, with an array of fine villas, chiefly owned by Germans. From the village a road leads towards the **Ponta de Garajau**, soon reaching a huge statue of Jesus (modelled on the famous one which overlooks Rio de Janeiro) erected in the 1920s by local Madeirans. The Ponta de Garajau is reputedly the place where the bodies of dead Protestant were flung into the sea in the days when Portuguese law forbad the burial of non-Catholics in Madeiran soil, a 'custom' which ended only when English settlers established the English Cemetery in Funchal. Some visitors assume the statue is related to this unfortunate practice, but that is not so: the reason for its raising is not known, having been to fulfil a secret promise by the locals. The view from the statue, and the headland, is superb, taking in the entire Funchal bay. The view downwards is equally impressive, the cliffs falling sheer for almost 200m (over 600ft). The local coves - many of them taken over by villa owners, but there are enough to almost guarantee you finding an empty one - are delightful. The beaches are rocky, and sometimes adorned with prickly pear cactus, but the sea is spectacularly clear.

Back on ER 204, the next place is Caniço, though to explore it you will need to leave the main road. Unlike Garajau, Caniço is a town, with an existence beyond tourism. It occupies both banks of a little river which, anciently, divided eastern and western Madeira, a division which seems faintly ludicrous now, but which was hugely significant at the time as the governors of the two Madeira's - João Gonçalves Zarco of the west (which he ruled from Funchal) and Tristão Vaz Teixeira to the east (which he ruled from Machico) - ruled them virtually as separate provinces. The two halves of Caniço were therefore separately administered and churches were built on either side of the river. Only in the eighteenth century was this situation rationalised. At that time the two churches were demolished and a new one built, this explaining the curious dedication to the Holy Spirit and St Anthony. The church has a superb bell tower in contrasting grey stone and whitewash. The church stands in the town's lovely main square with its patterned basalt paving. Nearby, the Capela da Madre de Deus dates from the early sixteenth century and has a beautiful Manueline doorway.

From the town, head towards the coast to reach the **Quinta Splendida**, an old mansion standing in well-tended gardens. The mansion has been recently converted into a hotel, but one as splendid as the name as it is part-furnished with antiques. The gardens can be visited, a visit being worthwhile for the view of the coast at least. Beyond the mansion is the hotel and beach complex of Caniço de Baixo. The sea offshore of the coast from Ponta da Oliveira, near the complex, to Ponta de Garajau has recently been declared a maritime reserve (the Reserva Natural Parcial do Garajau) set up to protect the sea life and shoreline.

Beyond Caniço the main road swings beneath the Pico de Agua, to the north (left) then passes a turning, also on the left, to **Moinhos**, named for a sugar mill that was the first to have been built on the island, before reaching the coast. The road then follows the coast closely, offering magnificent views of the sea, to the right, and of the fertile country, to the left, once used for growing bananas and vegetables, but now largely uncultivated and returning to the wild. Follow this fine road to Santa Cruz, a village perched at the end of Madeira's airport runway.

Santa Cruz

Santa Cruz is indeed one of the oldest settlements on the island, a church having been built here in the mid-fifteenth century. From this church a tombstone (which experts date to about 1470) survives in the new church, built in 1533 on the old site. The church is one of the best preserved from that period on the island and is well worth visiting. Externally the church is simple and dignified, its doorway flanked by a very unusual pair of buttresses. The doorway and small rose window above it are carved in the distinctive Manueline style. The short, sturdy tower served as a refuge for the townsfolk in the event of pirate attack. Inside the church there is the old tombstone and a number of Seville-made *azulejos* from the convent of Nossa Senora da Piedade which was demolished to make way for the airport. The stone slab in the floor of the choir is said to cover the grave of the church's original benefactor, João de Freitas. The church is also unusual in having aisles with excellent stone arches, which make it very wide. In

The Naming of Santa Cruz

In 1654 Francisco Manuel de Melo, a Portuguese writer, published a story telling of the illicit love between a man and woman at the court of England's Edward III. Sir Robert Machin, a minor nobleman and the hero of the tale, falls in love with Anna d'Arfet (probably a corruption of Anne of Hereford). But Anna is betrothed to a nobleman of greater rank, and when her father discovers that she returns Sir Robert's love he persuades the king to throw Machin into gaol. Sir Robert escapes, sends a message to Anna and the pair elope, boarding a ship for France. But the ship is blown off course and, ultimately, lands on Madeira. Sir Robert and Anna are entranced by the island and do not notice that the ship, restocked with water and some food, has set sail again. It fares no better on its second journey, being blown on to the Moroccan shore where the crew is captured and imprisoned. Sir Robert and Anna live an idyllic life on Madeira, but soon Anna falls ill and dies. Sir Robert buries his love, placing a cross on her grave and calling the place it lies Santa Cruz, after the cross. Sir Robert then makes a raft on which he sets sail. He, too, is blown to Morocco where he is imprisoned with a captured Portuguese. He tells the man of Madeira, but then dies. The man's friends raise a ransom for his release and he returns to Portugal to tell the royal court of the island.

This version of the legendary discovery of Madeira differs subtly from the earliest version (see the Introduction), but does offer a romantic, if sad, reason for the town's name.

---

fact, the church is the largest on the island outside of Funchal.

Close to the church is the Town Hall, built in 1513 and one of the best surviving examples of secular Manueline architecture on the island. The date of its construction is known exactly because until the early nineteenth century it was carved on to the façade. At that time, the town's authorities, had the date removed because they were ashamed that the building was so old!

Santa Cruz began life as a fishing port, and remains one, the tourist industry having largely bypassed it because of its position close to the airport. This seems a not entirely sensible decision: although aircraft do pass very close overhead, the traffic is not really sufficient to cause a major nuisance and the town is an excellent centre for those intending to make a holiday of touring the island. However, the lack of tourist development means that the town has retained its character, and this is nowhere better illustrated than in the market hall where the day's fishing catches are sold. A fish market may not be to everyone's liking, but the hall should still be visited for the beautiful azulejo mural near the entrance, by the Portuguese artist Oureiro Agueda.

Though there is little tourist development at Santa Cruz there is a good beach backed by recently planted palm trees with some facilities - toilets, changing rooms. It is worth a visit if only to see the dragon trees (*Dracaeno*

Praia do Natal Caniçal

draco), an oddly shaped tree with a bare trunk and a top-knot of multiple clusters of long, thin, grey-green leaves. The trees are indigenous to Madeira (and also to the Canaries and Cape Verde Islands) and acquired their name because, as with the rubber tree, the cut trunk bleeds a useful sap. In this case the sap, bright red and called dragon's blood, was a sought after dye. So sought after in fact that the tree that the tree was all but exterminated on the island. The Santa Cruz trees are one of the best remaining groups.

From Santa Cruz the road runs along the edge of the runway. Until the 1960s airborne visitors to Madeira landed at a military base on Porto Santo and were then ferried across to the main island. The original plan for Madeira's own airport envisaged one on a plateau high in the mountains, well away from towns and villages. Unfortunately the advantages of the site were outweighed by the disadvantage identified by several months spent collecting data at the new site: the airport would spend long periods fog-bound. The Santa Caterina site was therefore chosen. Initially it had a runway so short that only certain aircraft could use it, and the landing was claimed by pilots to be the most difficult and dangerous in Europe. A pillared extension – known, disparagingly, by the locals as the 'aircraft carrier' – has solved this problem, but a further extension is required so that the most modern jets can use the airport. Further extension is complicated by the fact that Madeira rises almost vertically out of the sea – go a hundred metres off-shore and the sea is amazingly deep. It is therefore

The Eastern Island

intended to swing the runway around to the north to limit the need for an extension over the water. The work is expected to be completed by 2000.

The road ducks under the runway, then meanders its way to Água de Pena, a small village that was once the anticipated centre of a tourist development, a development placed on hold (probably for ever) by the decision to re-align the airport runway. Turn right in the village to reach, after a short drive, a miradouro (viewpoint) named for Francisco Álvares de Nóbrega, one of Portugal's foremost eighteenth century poets who was born near Machico. The poet was notorious for producing verses lampooning the Catholic church, a course of action which led to imprisonment on the mainland. There he was tortured by the Inquisition and, rather than face further suffering, committed suicide. He was 34. History does not record whether De Nóbrega knew this spot, but if he did he must have found the view of Machico and the Ponta de São Lourenço inspirational.

Machico

Machico is claimed to have been named for Sir Robert Machin (see the Introduction, and Santa Cruz above) by João Gonçalves Zarco when he first landed on Madeira. Zarco is claimed to have found the graves of Machin and Anna d'Arfet, and to have named the spot in the Englishmen's honour. Of course, most versions of the story of Machin and his true love have Sir Robert escaping the island, so this version of the tale merely adds to the confusion over Madeira's true discovery. The idea of the town being named for Machin is romantic, but as Zarco was born in the Portuguese town of Monchique, it is possible that he actually named it for his home. Machico is Madeira's second largest town (after Funchal), with a population of about 12,000, and (also after the capital) the island's second largest tourist centre.

An exploration of Machico should start in **Largo do Município**, the town's main square, shaded by fine trees. Here there is a monument to Tristão Vaz Teixeira, co-founder of Madeira as a Portuguese island, and the governor of the eastern region when it was split into two. Teixeira's wife, Branca, is credited with having built the town's first church, the **Igreja da Nossa Senhora da Conceição** (Our Lady of the Conception) which overlooks the square. Branca Teixeira must have been a persuasive lady as she talked King Manuel I into substantial benefactions to the church. The most notable was the statue of the Virgin and Child which can be seen in Funchal's Museum of Sacred Art. The king also donated the south doorway, which is a superb example of the Manueline in style. Inside the church there are other fine Manueline features: some carvings near the doorway and the arched entrance to the Teixeira chapel - the Teixeira's coat-of-arms forms part of the arch.

Close to the church - along a narrow street heading off towards the sea: there are two streets heading that way, to reach the right one follow Teixeira's gaze - is a famous Machico landmark. No 15 is a typical Madeiran wine shop with a window display which includes bottles - suitably dusty and cobweb hung - dating back to the 1840s. Con-

> ### The Chapel of Miracles
>
> When the chapel was destroyed by the floods of 1803 all its contents were washed out to sea. Days later an American ship off Madeira saw something floating in the water. When they retrieved it the crew found it was a wooden crucifix. They took it ashore at Machico where the discovery was hailed as a miracle. A new chapel was built and on 8 October 1815 the Crucifix was carried into it in procession. The procession is repeated each year on 8 October, the 9 October being a local holiday. In the procession those who are seeking help in the curing of diseases from the miraculous Crucifix carry models of the afflicted part of their body made in wax. Inside the chapel the discovery of the Crucifix is the subject of a large painting.

tinue towards the sea to reach Rua Dr Almada. Turn right here to reach the town's Tourist Information Office which is housed in the cream low-walled **Fortaleza de Nossa Senhora do Amparo**, one of three fortresses built in Machico during the early years of the eighteenth century to protect the town from pirate raids. The fortress is curious in being triangular in shape (a design said to have been used to increase the number of cannons facing the sea while limiting the length of the walls). The Mercado Velho restaurant opposite the entrance o the fort is an excellent place for lunch or a coffee.

A second fortress (the **Fortaleza da Sao João Batista**) can be seen at the far end of the Cais, the quay on the northern area of Machico's bay. That fortress is now a private house. The peak above the castle is **Pico do Facho**, the peak of the torch, so called because a beacon fire was lit on its summit if pirates were spotted. The third fortress did not survive one of the terrible floods which have plagued the town throughout its history.

On the far side of the river from Largo do Município, just off the small square of Largo dos Milagres, is the **Capela dos Milagres**, the Chapel of Miracles, whose name derives from one of these periodic floods. The site is believed to be that on which the first chapel ever built on Madeira was raised by Zarco soon after he had laid claim to the island. The site was not a secure one, though the first chapel is claimed to have burnt down, a subsequent one was destroyed by flooding in 1803.

Close to the mouth of the river (on the town side) is the **Lota**, as the local fish market is known. As elsewhere on Madeira, the market is worth visiting in the early morning when the day's catch is auctioned. Now follow the harbour wall away from the river, passing the football stadium (Machico has one of Madeira's best teams) to reach the **Capela de São Roque**, beyond the unmistakable Dom Pedro Hotel. The chapel is built over a miraculous spring and is dedicated to the Italian St Rocca who helped victims of the Black Death in Rome. When he caught the disease himself he was miraculously cured. The dedication in Machico probably followed an outbreak of plague, though

Whaling

The whalers of Caniçal were the true successors of the men that Herman Melville wrote of in Moby Dick, for not only were they the last to hunt with hand-held harpoons and spears from small open boats (as opposed to the huge factory ships armed with huge guns firing harpoons tipped with explosives) but they also hunted the sperm whale. The sperm whale is the largest of the toothed whales, males reaching up to 20m (65ft) in length and 40 tons in weight, though the average male is more likely to be 15m (50ft), and females smaller again. The whale is also renowned, in reality as well as in myth, for smashing the boats of the men who hunted it and is probably responsible for more deaths than any other species. When

John Huston was filming his version of Moby Dick, he came to Madeira to film real hunts. All the whaling sequences in the final film (apart from three involving Moby Dick himself, a large plastic model) involve Madeiran whalers.

The open boat method of killing whales was extremely cruel. The harpoon, with its long line of thick rope which was attached to the prow of the boat, very rarely killed the whale, merely causing it enough pain and damage to quickly exhaust it. The wounded whale would dive to escape the torment, but being air-breathing would need to surface, when it did it was harpooned again. Eventually the whale's suffering would prevent further diving and the boat would draw alongside so that spears could be thrust into its heart for the final kill. The hunt (and, therefore, the animal's death) was a protracted affair and was impossible to condone even by those who saw modern whaling as acceptable. But in addition to being an exercise in cruelty (and bravery too, it has to be admitted: the Caniçal whalers were a special breed who risked death on every trip) the hunting also severely depleted the numbers of sperm and other whales which had once been numerous around the island.

Finally, in June 1981 the hunting stopped, hopefully for good. To further aid conservation of the remaining whales and the recovery of numbers a reserve was set up around the island, encompassing 200,000 square kilometres (72,000 square miles) of sea. In the old days men would sit on top Pico do Facho watching for the tell-tale blow of whales (as their ancestors had watched for the sails of pirate ships). Hopefully in the not too distant future such spray plumes will again be a future of Madeiran seascapes.

107

the miraculous properties of the spring seem to pre-date the building. The chapel has a series of superb *azulejos* depicting scenes from the saint's life.

Ponta de São Lourenço

From Machico the main road (ER 108) follows the river valley, heading inland, but another road (ER 109) branches right to reach Caniçal and the narrow peninsula of Ponta de São Lourenço.

Until the 1950s **Caniçal** was isolated from the rest of Madeira, reached only by boat or along mountain walk. A tunnel was then driven to take ER 109 to the village. At the same time a *levada* was constructed in the hope of developing some agriculture in an otherwise arid area. Caniçal was the centre of Madeiran whaling, a trade which stopped in the early 1980s, and is today most notable for its whaling museum (the Museu da Baleia). Although the collection, with its harpoons and spears, details the grisly business of slaughtering whales, the video (in English) explains the part now played by the old Madeiran whalers in helping with whale conservation. The Caniçal whalers were a help to scientists attempting to piece together the lifecycle of the sperm whale. The museum's most instructive exhibits are a full size model of a sperm whale and an actual Madeiran whaling boat. Horrific though the trade was, there is little doubt that the whalers were brave men. The museum also includes a collection of scrimshaw (carved and engraved whale teeth and bone). Scrimshaw and small models of the whaling boats can be bought here or at the little shop across from the museum where an old whaler carves.

After the cessation of whaling the Madeiran government attempted to bring new industries to the area by creating a Zona Franca, a free-trade area near the village, an experiment which has not been a success either in economic or environmental terms. As a result, most of the village men are still seafarers, a walk along the beach past the hauled-up, colourful tuna boats being the other highlight of a visit. A beach walk eastwards soon reaches the whaling station where the animals were butchered. It now houses the village fish market.

As well as the pebbly beach on to which the fishing boats are hauled, Caniçal has another, called Prainha and about 2.5km (1.5 miles) to the east, which is the only truly sandy beach (a very dark sand) on Madeira and, as a result, is popular with locals and some visitors from Machico. On the old volcanic cone which rises above the beach is the **Capela da Senhora da Piedade**, a chapel housing a sixteenth century statue of the Virgin. In late September the statue is taken to Caniçal and then transported back to the chapel in procession, the first part of the procession being by water, the Virgin being accompanied by the village fishing fleet.

The Prainha beach lies on the narrow, twisting isthmus of **Ponta de São Lourenço**, a wild peninsula of steep cliffs and sculpted hills. The road continues past the beach, eventually ending above a semi-circular bay, Porta da Abra: the curious structures in the sea are fish farms. At several points along the way there are viewpoints of the southern edge of the peninsula, and short walks also lead to viewpoints of the northern edge. The northern edge is the more dramatic, the view taking in purple cliffs (up to 200m - 650ft - high) splashed with green vegetation when they are angled back from sheer, with the swirling waters of the Atlantic bashing away at their bases. Periodically the sea wins a victory in the perpetual war it wages against the cliffs, huge sections breaking off to litter the narrow shore at the cliff base before being broken up and dispersed by the pounding waters. There could hardly be a greater contrast between luscious, exotic gardens of Funchal and this seascape, another reminder of the range of delights on Madeira.

In spring, the difference between the two Madeiras is less apparent, rain coaxing the peninsula into flower making it bloom, briefly, with a mixture of thistles, poppies and other colourful wild flowers. It is believed that originally the peninsula was almost entirely wooded, but that the trees were felled and domestic and feral sheep and goats grazed attempted regrowth away. Now a nature reserve is to be set up to try to return part, at least, of the peninsula to its original form.

From the road end a path (see chapter on Madeira Walks) leads to the best viewpoint of the north coast and on to the very tip of the peninsula. From there the near view is of the Ilhéu do Fora, just a couple of hundred metres away, with its lighthouse, while a clear day allows a distant view of Porto Santo, to the north-east, and the Desertas islands to the south-east.

Machico to Funchal: the inland route

From Machico, take ER 108, heading along the valley of the Machico river, its acacia trees pale yellow with blossom in the spring. Soon there is a choice of routes. A left turn leads to Santo da Sera, a very worthwhile visit, while ahead is the Portela Pass which is also worth visiting and from which another detour leads to Porto da Cruz. In a long day all these places can be fitted in.

Santo da Serra is really Santo António da Serra, but that name rarely appears, even on maps of the island. Standing almost 700m (2,300ft) above sea level, the village is pleasantly cool after Machico, and was once a favourite mountain retreat for English traders, some of whom built mansions here. The most spectacular of these is Quinta da Serra (also known as Quinta da Junta) which was built by the Blandy family. Today the mansion is owned by the Madeiran government, and while the building is not open to the public, the extensive parkland which surrounds it is. It is a lovely park, with formal gardens and a venues of azaleas and camellias. There are tennis courts and a children's playground, and a small zoo. A path leads through a wilder section of park, with fine trees, to the Miradouro dos Ingleses. This is aptly named as the viewpoint really was the work of the English, the Blandy family having had it cut so that a look-out could scan the horizon for ships. Today's visitor can enjoy the same view, though with a more relaxed eye, taking in the marvellous panorama which extends from Machico to Ponte de São Lourenço.

The Wicker Work of Camacha

It is unclear when wickerwork became a Madeiran craft, there being the usual conflicting stories. It is often said that William Hinton, an English trader - and ancestor of the lad who brought a football to the island - developed the craft seen today, introducing not only the idea itself, bringing examples of English wickerwork to Madeira after seeing the potential of the island's willow trees, but the business aspects of the trade. It may well be that Hinton developed the craft, but whether he introduced it is open to doubt. It is known for instance, that the builders of the first levadas used a wicker seat at the end of a rope to descend sheer cliffs - the seat being more comfortable than a rope around the waist, but no less intimidating if the drop was sufficiently long - and the Madeiran farmers used a large, plate-shaped wicker basket (barreleiro) during planting and harvesting, and also to carry stones if they were building a hut. These plate-shaped baskets were later taken up by house builders in town, and are still used by farmers to bring produce to market. Madeirans also tell the story of an islander imprisoned on the mainland who learned the craft from a Portuguese cell-mate, but that may be a tongue-in-cheek tale.

The wicker workers of Camacha, who make up the majority of Madeira's several thousand craftsmen, use canes from the Salix alba, the white willow, which grows close to the village and in the valleys cutting inland from the northern coast. Having their heads in the clouds help the willows to grow canes up to 2m (6.5ft) in length in a single season. The canes are cut early in the year (January to March), the pollarded willow then re-growing during the next summer. After cutting there are two methods for producing workable canes. Most canes are peeled and then boiled, this producing a workable cane quickly and giving the canes their characteristic golden colour. A longer process soaks the canes in cold water, often for months. This produces a white cane, but is an expensive process and is only used for special orders.

Once the canes are ready the craftworkers begin. As with embroidery this is a cottage industry, with both men and women weaving the canes (though most workers are men). Visitors to Camacha will often pass houses with open doors, the weaver sitting just inside so that he can occasionally stop work to watch the world go by. Usually the workers are happy for visitors to watch. The workers make an assortment of goods, from baskets to cane furniture and occasionally, just for fun, birds and animals, including deer with can antlers. As with embroidery, the trade is regulated by IBTAM (the Instituto de Bordados, Tapeçãria e Artesanto de Madeira - the Madeiran Institute of Embroidery, Tapestry and Handicrafts) and visitors should look for their seal to ensure they are getting the genuine article. At one time small baskets were also made from canes cut from broom, a thinner cane which could be used to produce a more delicate product. Broom canes are rarely used today, but imported baskets of the material are for sale on the island. They are clearly marked as such in Camacha's Café Rególio, but visitors elsewhere should look for the IBTAM seal to avoid being passed off with imported broom, or with Chinese willow cane work. It is also worth remembering that the cane 'sofa' which looks so wonderful in the showroom will not look quite as good a buy at the airport check-in desk.

The boom in wickerwork in Victorian times was repeated after the 1939-45 war when cane furniture was again in vogue. A slump followed, but there has been a revival lately.
In remains to be seen whether wickerwork can remain a major Madeiran employer in the face of competition from the cheaper work made in China and Poland.

Santo do Serra has a quiet central square and a neat church. It is claimed that the priest here was instrumental in the setting up of the Museum of Sacred Art in Funchal when he fetched a couple of lengths of timber from the church to place under the wheels of a visitor's car which was threatening to sink in axle-deep mud. The visitor realised the boards were actually paintings. He took then away, had them cleaned and examined, and it was discovered they were sixteenth century Flemish masterpieces. The find resulted in Madeira's village churches being scoured for similar works. It is a nice tale (and one that is often told) but seems extremely unlikely. Indeed, it seems more likely to be a calculated insult to the priest's intelligence. Many Madeirans still swear by its authenticity, but I remain to be convinced.

Much more credible (a fact, in fact) is that the village's golf course was the first on Madeira. It now has a new clubhouse, but the old one - now disused - is much more attractive, its little tower decorated with an art nouveau frieze.

ER 108 - or the road heading west from Santo de Serra - climbs to reach **Portela**, a hamlet near the high pass of the road. There is a restaurant at the pass, one which must have been very welcome to travellers climbing up the steep hill from the northern coast. It is still a good spot to stop. If the weather is clear it is a wonderful viewpoint of **Porto da Cruz** and Penha de Águia (Eagle Rock), the huge, steep-sided, but flat-topped rock mass to the west (left as you look) of the town. Despite its forbidding appearance the Rock - it is 590m (1,935ft) above sea level - can be climbed along a narrow, vertiginous path that, in spring, is completely overgrown by flesh-ripping vegetation. The local Madeiran walkers then clear the path, so summer climbers will have an easier time - but it is no place for those who do not care for big drops.

From Portela a detour drops down to the north coast. Porto da Cruz is a very old settlement, but the prosperous days of the sugar industry are now long gone: one sugar mill remains - it is also a distillery for aguardente, Madeiran rum. The sea front offers a quiet walk and a chance to watch the waves, but there is little else to detain the visitor. Much the same is true of nearby São Roque

Places to Visit

Quinta Splendida
Caniço
Open: All year, daily 9am-dusk
☏ 934027

Museu da Baleia (Whaling Museum)
Caniçal
Open: All year, Tuesday-Sunday 10am-12noon and 1-6pm,
☏ 961407

Quinta da Serra
Santo da Serra
Open: At any reasonable time

Café Relógio
Largo Achada
Camacha
Open: All year, daily except public holidays 9am-8pm
☏ 922114

do Faial, though its peace and quiet make a short walk worthwhile. Close to the village a stream tumbles over a picturesque waterfall into pools which the locals claim are bottomless.

From Portela, ER 102 heads south, back to Funchal. The road winds through pleasant, but not spectacular, country with forests on the higher land and willow trees in more sheltered areas. This is a fruit and vegetable growing area, but the farmers supplement their income by selling willow sticks to the wicker makers of Camacha, the next big village. As you approach the village you will see bundles of willow canes outside some of the houses. As with Madeira's embroidery industry, wickerwork is a cottage industry.

Camacha is a quiet, unassuming village with few highlights - apart from its wickerwork - but a gentle air that repays any attention it receives. Many visitors get no further than the main square, the Largo da Archada, but those who venture further will be rewarded with a glimpse of the old Madeira: the village church is eighteenth century and houses an extraordinary wooden chandelier. Closer to the main square, the village hall is home to one of the island's best folk bands - they are so good they frequently play away from the village, but can often be found in the Café Relógio on Saturday evenings.

In the main square a plaque records the fact that the first game of football ever to have been played on Portuguese soil took place in the village, the instigator being Harry Hinton, the student son of an English resident, who brought a ball back on a vacation from college in 1875 and taught the local lads the rules.

At the edge of the square the Café Relógio (Clock Café) is not only a good café and restaurant, but a showroom for the local wickerworkers. The café was built as a mansion by an English wine trade - a fact that might explain the clock tower, which has echoes of Big Ben. The clock was another gift of Dr Michael Grabham, physician, naturalist and horologist.

Finally, before leaving Camacha, enjoy the marvellous panorama of the east coast from the viewpoint beside the café.

From Camacha the roads winds through fruit orchards and clumps of wild hydrangea. About 3km (2 miles) after ER 102 and ER 203 join - and after the turn, on the left, for Blandy's Garden - there is a fine viewpoint on the left-hand side. It is the last one before the road drops down into Funchal, passing the Botanical Gardens on the way to the city centre.

6. Porto Santo and the Desertas

Opposite: Passeios , Porto Santo

Porto Santo

Porto Santo

Porto Santo lies just 40km (25 miles) to the north-east of Madeira, yet seems as though it must be many more, so great is the physical contrast between the two. Madeira is lush green and studded with colourful flowers, a tribute to its rainfall and rivers. Porto Santo is brown and arid, desert-like in comparison. As well as a geographical distance which belies the true closeness, Porto Santo also seems to be a change to a different time frame. The inhabitants are the butt of cruel Madeiran humour which portrays them as lazy and slow-witted. The Madeirans call the Porto Santo islanders profetas, prophets, the name deriving from a curious incident in the sixteenth century. Then, one resident, sometimes called Fernão Nunes, sometimes Fernão Bravo (Fernando the Brave, thought to have been a fearless Portuguese knight who settled on Porto Santo after a distinguished military career), declared himself a messenger from God. With his young niece he toured the island, showing an uncanny knack for telling island folk the intimate secrets (some they were not keen to have advertised) of their pasts and reminding them of the need to live sin-free lives. The pair soon had a following sufficient to disturb the established church and soldiers were sent from Madeira to arrest the 'prophets'.

The islanders do not seem to view the nickname as an insult - though it might be a good idea not to test this out with too much enthusiasm - and the local (rather good) pop group has even called itself Profetas.

When you get to know the Porto Santo islanders, the Madeiran idea of them is seen to be false, though there is without doubt a difference in tempo between the islands. On Madeira - not everywhere, but certainly in Funchal and the other larger towns, which means most of the population - there is constant movement, while on Porto Santo there is relaxed attitude to life which could occasionally make somnambulism seem hyperactive. If someone was to run across the main square in Vila Baleira you could be forgiven for thinking there was a fire. It is not to everyone's liking of course. Those who come to Madeira keen to enjoy a (relatively) hectic nightlife might find Porto Santo a frustratingly dull place. The same would be true of those who came to enjoy Madeira's gardens and visited the smaller island expecting more of the same. But for those seeking a quiet relaxation from the endless bustle of modern life, and a beach on which to enjoy it, Porto Santo is the answer. If your life seems to require more hours in each day, this little island is the place to go shopping. Spare time is available in such abundance here you feel you could parcel it up and take it home with you.

Porto Santo: A Short History

Porto Santo means the holy harbour and is first seen on charts which pre-date the official discovery of the island by many years. It seems likely that explorers or traders working the coast of Africa had sometimes be driven out into the Atlantic by storms and had found shelter in the lee of the island, naming it for the gift from God which it must have seemed. Later travellers, after the island's vegetation had been stripped, called it, disparagingly, the 'brown island', a name which is still heard occasionally causing the local Tourist Office to start to term it *Ilhéu Dourada*, the golden island, a rather brave attempt to turn an insult to advantage.

The island was settled soon after its first discovery, Bartolomeu Perestrelo being granted the governorship when his more illustrious travelling companions, João Gonçalves Zarco and Tristão Vaz Teixeira, moved on to the larger neighbour. Perestrelo's family was granted the governorship in perpetuity, but held office only through half-a-dozen generations (and the occasional mishap, one Governor Perestrelo being executed for the murder of his wife). The island found by the early settlers was heavily wooded, chiefly with dragon trees and juniper, but these were cleared for the planting of sugar and vines, and regrowth was halted by rabbits which were deliberately set free. In the absence of vegetation the wind blew the fertile soil into the sea, and in the absence of the soil (which held moisture like a sponge), the island

Christopher Columbus, Porto Santo and Madeira

There are few established facts linking Columbus to Madeira, but those that do exist suggest that he must have spent time here. The claims that his Madeiran interlude sowed the seed of the idea of a voyage to the New World is still the subject of claim and counter-claim.

Christopher Columbus was born in Genoa, probably in 1451, arriving in Lisbon at the age of about 25 as an ambitious young sailor. At the time there were a number of Genoese sailors working in Portugal and perhaps through them Columbus was commissioned to sail to Madeira in 1478 to buy sugar. In 1479 he married Filipa Moniz Perestrelo, the daughter of the Governor of Porto Santo. The marriage has perplexed historians for many years. How did a mere sailor acquire the hand of a noble-born woman? Some have noted that Perestrelo and Columbus shared a common ancestry in the Italian city of Piacenza and that this might have played a part. Others conjecture that Filipa might have had an affair and so become a liability to here father who, unable to marry her to a nobleman, was glad to have her taken off his hands.

It is possible that Columbus was keener on Filipa's connections than on her as his true love, some historians believing that he was already seeking noble patronage, and possibly even trying to establish himself as a leading player in the Dragon's Blood trade - the sap from the Dracaena palm (dragon trees) being a sought-after dye. Porto Santo is known to have had a large number of dragon trees at the time. It is thought that Columbus and his wife lived on Porto Santo and in Funchal, but there is no real evidence for either. The Casa de Columbus in Vila Baleira is claimed to have been the Porto Santo house, but seems to be at least a century younger than the required age.

In 1480 or 1481 the couple had a son, but his birthplace is unknown. It is known that from 1484 Columbus was trying to persuade the Portuguese royal family to finance a voyage west across the Atlantic: finally when all his attempts failed, he offered his services to the Spanish crown and it was from Spain that he set out on his voyage to the New World in 1492.

Until they realised the tourist potential of Columbus, the Madeirans treated the subject with disdain. Now, old legends about the usefulness the islands to the explorer have resurfaced. It is said that Columbus' examinations of seeds and plants washed up on the western shore of Porto Santo were instrumental in forming his view that there was land (probably India) across the ocean. It is claimed that charts held by the Perestrelo family, and accessible to him after his marriage to Filipa, hinted at the existence of the New World. And it is also claimed that on Porto Santo and Madeira Columbus spoke with sailors whose ships had been blown across the Atlantic by storms and had already landed in the Americas. The truth, or otherwise, of these stories will never be known.

Praia, Porto Santo

turned into a semi-desert. Today an attempt is being made, close to the airport especially, at re-afforestation.

Sadly almost all the dragon trees have gone and what little soil remains grows little but a few figs, vines, melons and pumpkins, and grass to support sheep and a few cows. Almost all the island's water is produced by desalination. Ironically, of the little natural water, one spring, producing a mineral-rich water, is believed to have medicinal properties and its water is bottled and exported to Madeira.

Porto Santo: A Tour

The visitor will land at the airport - whose huge runway, longer than Madeira's, almost cuts the island in half - or dock at the little port. Either way the first step will be Vila Baleira, the main town, where most of Porto Santo's population of 4,000 live.

Vila Baleira

The town's main square, **Largo do Pelourinho**, is the ideal place to catch your breath after the journey from Madeira and to settle down to Porto Santo's pace of life. Dragon and olive trees, and a few tall date palms, offer shade, and there are several good cafes.

When you are ready to explore you will find that most of the worthwhile sites are just a few steps away. The **Church of Nossa Senhora da Piedade** was first built in the early fifteenth century, but was pillaged and burned several times by pirates. The present building dates from 1667, after the last pirate attack. It has interesting *azulejos* on the outside and several clock faces, perhaps a subtle joke on the slow pace of life. Nearby, the **Town Hall** is older, though it, too, has required partial rebuilds.

Now go along the street beside the church to reach the **Casa de Colombo**, the house claimed to have been the home of Christopher Columbus and now a museum to him. The museum has a collection of furniture and seafaring equipment from Columbus' time, together with maps and charts depicting the history of the discovery of new lands beyond Europe, and tracing the route of Columbus' voyage. There is also a conjectural history of Columbus on Porto Santo.

A Tour of the Island

From Vila Baleira it is a short stroll to Porto Santo's main attraction, **Campo de Baixo** - the white sand beach which extends virtually the whole length of the island's southern coast, a distance of 9km (5.5 miles). Apart from August, when the Madeirans arrive in numbers, the beach is usually empty (or, at least, has so few people in comparison to its size that it seems empty). As the sea is warm throughout the year, and Porto Santo does not have the cloud cover Madeira occasionally experiences, it is worth spending time here. The other reason for a lazy hour or a stroll is the chance of finding someone buried in the sand. The islanders believe the beach's sand has healing properties and many take an occasional 'cure' by being buried up to their necks in it.

Heading west from Vila Baleira, there is little to hold the interest. **Campo de Cima** has an array of fine villas and a few, now mostly ruinous, windmills, while at the island's tip, Ponta da Calheta, there is a pleasant view of the uninhabited Ilhéu de Baxio. On clear days Madeira and the Desertas islands can be seen from here. On the flank of the Pico de Ana Ferreira which sits above the little hamlet of Ponta, near **Ponta da Calheta** is the Capela de São Pedro, built in the late seventeenth century. It is opened only once each year for a service on St Peter's Day (29 June).

The northern/eastern end of **Porto** Santo is the more interesting part, and a circular road visits the best of the sites. Heading north from Vila Baleira a turn right soon reaches the base of Pico de Castelo, named for the fortress which once crowned it, erected to offer the islanders some protection against pirates.

Porto Santo

The Rare Monk Seal

When the first settlers reached Madeira there were large colonies of monk seals there. Indeed, so notable were the colonies that one village - Câmara de Lobos - is named for the seal (which is known as the lobo do mar, sea wolf, in Portuguese). But the Madeira fishermen saw the seal as a competitor and slaughtered them. Soon there were seals only on the Desertas Islands, and even there they were not safe, the fishermen once having organised a raiding party which is thought to have slaughtered at least half the remaining animals. Today there are perhaps 50 seals left, and these are totally protected.

The monk seal is, to be precise, the Mediterranean monk seal (Monachus monacus) to distinguish it from two other members of the same family (the Caribbean monk seal, now though to be extinct, and the Hawaiian monk seal). The Mediterranean monk is highly endangered, with just a few animals remaining in small colonies in the Aegean and the Sea of Marmara, as well as here in the Atlantic. It is about 2.5m (8ft) long and weighs about 350kg, dark brown in colour, though lighter underneath and with a white belly patch. The seals eat fish and octopus, taking them from relatively shallow water as they are not great divers.

The walk to the top of the peak from the road end takes about 15 minutes, and is worthwhile for the view. Porto Santo is a small island, only 12km (7.5 miles) long and never more than 5km (3 miles) wide, and from **Pico do Castelo** almost all of it can be seen. The view to the north-east is cut short by the island's highest peak, Pico de Facho - 517m (1,696ft) - named for the 'torch' or beacon which would be lit here if pirates were spotted. The beacon was to warn the islanders, but was also useful as an early warning to Madeirans because often the pirates would move on to the larger island after attacking Porto Santa, the smaller island being an appetiser for the main course, a place to get your eye in, as it were.

Beyond the turn to Pico do Castelo is Camacha, where one of the island's windmills has been preserved. With its stone bases, wooden turrets and cloth sails the windmills is extremely attractive. Such windmills were used as corn mills when cereals could still be grown on the island. Close to the mill is a very ancient house, typical of the old Porto Santo style, its walls being of stones without mortar, its roof of clay on wooden beams. The house is now a fine restaurant.

Close to Camacha is the Fonte da Areira where water springs from a landscape of weird sandstone sculptures, the work of the wind and rain. Like the beach's sand, the spring water is claimed to have medicinal properties. But not only that: it is also claimed to be the secret of eternal youth.

From Camacha the road circles the high peaks, passing through two hamlets - Serra de Dentro (now deserted) and Serra de Fora - before reaching the **Portela** viewpoint from where there is a superb view of the beach and of the Ilhéu de Cima, another uninhabited island (but with a lighthouse) off the island's eastern tip. Close to the viewpoint is the **Capela Nossa Senhora da Graça**, built in the 1950s but on the site of a fifteenth chapel which is said to have been erected where the Virgin Mary appeared to a group of islanders. The chapel is the scene of an important procession and service on Assumption day.

The Desertas Islands

About 20km (12 1/2 miles) to the southeast of Madeira lie the three islands of the Desertas - Ilhéu Chao, Desertas Grande and Bugio. There have been spasmodic attempts to settle Deserta Grande, the largest of the islands, but these have all been defeated by the lack of water, the pitifully thin soil and the island's narrowness, a fact which means that almost any storm results in damage to buildings or crops. After the last attempted settlement, a couple of centuries ago (after the folk left the islands were 'Deserted'), the island's became a privately owned retreat on which honoured guests could hunt feral goats and rabbits. More recently the islands have been declared a Nature Reserve, chiefly for the protection of the monk seal, and are off limits to all except accredited research scientists.

It is, however, possible to join cruises around the islands and very, very rarely groups are allowed ashore. If you are lucky beware *Lycosa ingens*, a large black spider with a reputation for being aggressive and a bite which has caused fatalities. Those on round tour cruises do not have to brave the spider. They may see the seals, and will also see some of the seabirds which use the islands for breeding. These include Cory's, Manx and little shearwaters and Bulwer's petrel. Bugio is also the nesting place of several pairs of the rare Fea's petrel (*Pterodroma feae*), a bird which, in flight, is indistinguishable from the equally rare Zino's petrel (Pterodroma madeira) which breeds in the Madeiran mountains. These two petrels have only recently been seen as sub-species, having previously been seen as a single species called the soft-plumaged petrel.

Selvagens

About 285km (180 miles) south of Madeira lies another group of island which form part of the Madeiran autonomous region, if not of its archipelago. There are two main islands and a number of islets, all uninhabited and forming a Nature Reserve for breeding seabirds. The Portuguese authorities have a manned station on the islands - a handful of men who are relieved every two weeks to prevent crushing boredom - to dissuade visitors, legends having it that the English pirate Captain Kidd buried the treasure looted from Lima Cathedral there. Several expeditions in the nineteenth century failed to find any trace of Kidd or his treasure, but the legend persists.

7. Walking on Madeira

There are few places in Europe which offer the visitor such a straightforward way of reaching its scenic highlights as Madeira. The *levada* system allows walkers to penetrate not only the beauties of the island's cultivated land and forests, but also to reach far up into the mountains. While it is true that the *levadas* present a few problems to inexperienced walkers - some sections being very exposed, and the paths being occasionally very slippery and (though less often) quite steep - they do overcome most of the difficulties of route finding. Only very occasionally is it necessary to cross from one *levada* to another, and if all else fails you can turn around and follow the water channel back to the start!

But as well as supplying the walker with the means of exploring, Madeira also demands exploration. If few other places are so easily walked, fewer still have walks which are so rewarding. Almost any walk into the heart of Madeira is worthwhile, and at their

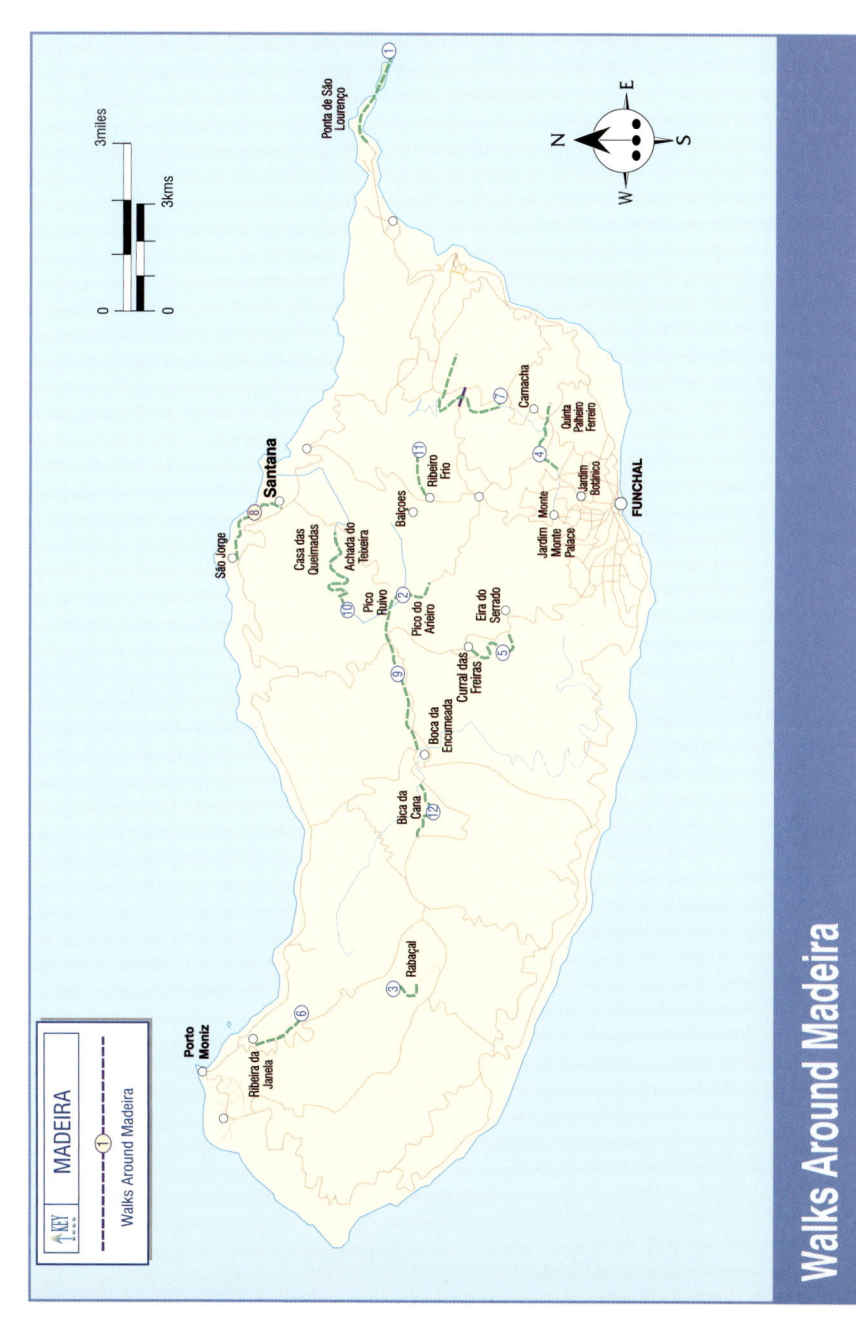

Opposite: Looking into the Janela Valley from the Levada do Risco

Walks Around Madeira

best the island's walks can, in the space of a few hours, lead the walker past the cultivated terraces, through wild forest studded with colourful flowers, offer a glimpse of wild, but beautiful, scenery – waterfalls and gorges – and finally reach a panoramic view of the mountains at the island's heart.

In the mountains, too, the walker is well catered for, engineered paths reaching, sometimes linking, the highest peaks. Such paths, and the following of water channels, may seem a desecration to those to whom the essence of a walk is an exploration of unspoilt country. But these things must be seen in context – the *levadas* exist to irrigate the land, their use allows the walker to penetrate country which would, otherwise, be off-limits to anyone not possessing a machete to hack a way through impenetrable forest, and the mountain paths are limited in number and allow casual walkers (rather than the totally committed) to enjoy the views from the highest peaks. Madeira's tallest mountains may not be of alpine proportions, but they are high enough, and Madeira's climate includes sudden changes, bringing down mist or a squall of rain: in such conditions experienced as well as inexperienced walkers will be happy to have a clear path to follow. And for the really experienced there are still enough areas of pathless wilderness.

Equipment

Good walking shoes or boots are essential. The waterfall and spring feeds of the *levadas* can make the going wet underfoot and without good footwear you may spend part of the walk with wet feet. The water can also make sections of the path, particularly on steep sections, very slippery. Madeira's soil makes a particularly slippery mud, and without a good tread you may have difficulty keeping your feet.

Long trousers are better than shorts and skirts as the undergrowth in the forest sections can occasionally attack the legs. A hat is also a good idea: the Madeiran sun can be very strong. For the same reason a good sunblock, waterproof to allow for sweating on uphill sections, is a must.

Always carry warm clothing and waterproofs. The Madeiran climate is changeable and may well offer you rain as well as a good view. The wind on the higher peaks can also be keen and if you are walking as the sun is going down the drop in temperature can take you by surprise.

A torch is essential. Many of the *levadas* have tunnelled sections and while these are never too long, and always straightforward, a missed step in the dark could lead to a soaking.

Carrying water on a hot day is a must. Dehydration reduces the body's efficiency dramatically, Some emergency food is also worthwhile – you are bound to meet your bus or taxi on time (but just in case....).

Finally, it almost goes without saying that walkers venturing out on to the wild moorland of Paúl de Sierra, or the land to the west of it, should have a map and compass.

Maps

Maps at scales to 1:25,000 are readily available in shops in Funchal.

Weather

Despite being relatively small, Madeira can sometimes offer an amazing variety of weather on a given day, and occasional large changes during the day too, the mountains creating a host of micro-climates. There are some general rules of thumb about the weather, but these tend to be useful for today rather than tomorrow, and it is usually best to make an early start, particularly for walks on the high peaks.

The 'rules' for local weather involve looking at the Desertas islands and they are rather more complicated than the standard idea that if you can see them it's going to rain and if you can't see them it is raining. In this case, if the islands are seen very clearly than the wind tends to be from the north-west. This usually means that most of Madeira will be clear, though there may be cloud in the east. If the Desertas are not only clearly visible but look much closer than usual, then the wind is probably from the south or south-west, a direction which brings rain, usually later today or tomorrow. If the Desertas are seen through haze, then the wind tends to be from the north or north-east. This usually means that eastern Madeira is cloudy, but most of the rest of the island is clear. Finally, if the Desertas are barely visible, or not visible, then the wind is usually easterly or south-easterly. If it is south-easterly then Madeira will be clear apart, possibly, from the south which may be cloudy. A true east wind, called the leste, blows from the Salve, a warm, moisture-free wind which brings ideal walking weather with a complete absence of cloud and wonderful visibility.

These 'rules' are, as with most rules, there to be broken, and Madeira's micro-climates makes them too imprecise to be of great value outside Funchal. The better idea is to watch the evening weather forecast, to ask at your hotel reception or, if your Portuguese is up to it, to ring 150 for the pre-recorded forecast.

Buses

As some of the walks given here are linear, walkers will need transport. Even walkers with their own transport may need a bus to return to their car. Madeira has a reasonably efficient bus system, though as with all such systems, the more remote the start or finish the less often do buses serving it run. The narrow, winding roads also mean that bus journeys take rather longer than might be imagined. For all the walks suggested here the bus (and/or taxi) options are given for the start and finish points, together with approximate times of service. This information should be checked before setting out on a walk as the bus companies (like private bus companies everywhere) can alter schedules with minimum notice. Below the names and colours of Madeiran buses are given. This is necessary as some of the companies run buses with identical numbers, to the occasional confusion of visitors. As an example, both Horãrios do Funchal and Sam run buses No. 113, one of which (Sam) serves Caniçal and the other does not.

Camacha/Horãrios do Funchal

Grey, Yellow and White or Yellow and White (but orange in Funchal)

Madeira

The summit of Bica da Cana

Waterfall near the Levada do Furado

Rabaçal

On the walk between Pico do Arieiro and Pico Ruivo

Caniço
Red, Cream and Grey

Rodoeste
Red, Cream and White

SAM
Green and Cream

São Roque do Faial
Red, White and Grey

A Selection of Walks

In this section a dozen walks are suggested which best explore Madeira's wonderful diversity of scenery - mountain walks, coastal walks, valley walks; walks along *levada*s and walks on engineered paths; walks offering magnificent views or scenic wonders.

All such selections are personal and are therefore open to criticism. To try to avoid some of the accusations of partiality the basis of selection is a list of thirteen walks published by the Madeiran Tourist Office. The office considers them to be the best on the island - and who are we to disagree? These walks tend to be on the high peaks (though they are not exclusively so), and so to redress the balance somewhat a small number of favourite valley walks has been included.

The times given for the walks does not include sightseeing or long stops for lunch etc.

1. Ponta da São Lourenço

The long finger of Ponta da São Lourenço is one of Madeira's most remarkable features and offers an exhilarating walk with magnificent views of coloured cliffs and sea stacks.

Start/Finish

The car park at the end of the road heading west from Caniçal. Caniçal is reached by SAM bus No. 113 from Funchal, an excellent service which runs more or less hourly (about every two hours at weekends) from 7am - 9pm. From the village a taxi is need to reach the car park.

Distance/Ascent

8km (5 miles), minimal climbing, though there is a sharp ascent at the end of the peninsula.

Time

About 3 hours.

Difficulties

Straightforward early in the walk, but later on there are exposed sections.

From the car park, follow the well-trodden path inland of the high viewpoint overlooking the Baía da Abra (Abra Bay), with magnificent views into and across it. After 15 minutes or so you go through a gap in an old stone wall. Just beyond there is a path fork: go left here for a short detour to the peninsula's northern coast from where there is a magnificent view of a pair of sea stacks, one reddish-brown and tortured by the crashing Atlantic, the other grey with a purplish sheen and still resisting all the sea's attempts to bring it down.

Return to the path fork and take the other branch, heading across bare rock. The route is marked by occasional real paint splashes, but the continuation can be seen beyond the rock: follow it through an area of oddly luxuriant plant life, with thistles and yellow poppies among clumps of feral cereals. The path is obvious, but telegraph poles and the occasional red marker still point the way. At one point there is a sharp climb downwards, the narrow ridge of rock being very exposed and a little awkward. It is the work of a few seconds to make the climb, but those nervous of the drop should think twice before attempting it.

Beyond the walk continue quite straightforwardly, with no more difficulties, climbing sharply to reach the actual tip of the peninsula, with a yawning drop (of around 150m - 500ft) and a marvellous view to the Ilhéu do Farol.

To return, reverse the outward route.

2. Pico de Arieiro and Pico Ruivo

Madeira's high peaks are an obvious objective for any walker. This exciting walk visits the summits of the island's highest and third highest mountains, and follows a line below the summit of the second highest.

Start/Finish

A difficult walk to accomplish as a linear journey as there is no public transport to either Pico do Arieiro or to Achada do Teixeira below Pico Ruivo. With a car the walk must be reversed. If two taxis are used, the second will collect you from Achada do Teixeira and take you to Santana or Faial for the São Roque do Faial buses to Funchal (Nos. 103 and 138 - 103 has early afternoon and late afternoon departures - late afternoon only on Sunday, 138 is morning only), or to Faial for 8am São Roque do Faial bus No. 53 which has one afternoon departure (but none on Saturday and Sunday)

Distance/Ascent

Pico de Arieiro - Pico Ruivo - Achada do Teixeira 5.5km (3.5 miles), about 500m (1,650ft) of ascent.

Pico de Arieiro - Pico Ruivo - Pico de Arieiro 8km (5 miles) about 800m (2,600ft) of ascent.

Time

Linear route 2^1/$_2$ hours. Return route 3^1/$_2$ hours.

Difficulties

A well trodden path, but still a major undertaking, the whole walk being at around 1,600 - 1,800 m (5,200-6,000ft) and susceptible to changeable (and sometimes harsh) weather.

Sometimes the path is destroyed by landslides. If a section of path is found to have been destroyed, please turn back. There are several tunnels along the way.

From Pico de Arieiro follow the broad, engineered path towards the angular peaks to the north. The path is good, but soon the ridge narrows, with sculpted chasms on each side: continue more comfortably to reach a viewpoint of the jagged peaks of the Pico das Torres (the Peak of Towers, Madeira's second highest peak). Continue below a cliff, with a superb view into the gorge of the Ribeiro do Cidrão and across to the Paúl da Serra. The path is now on a very narrow ridge of rock, with a handrail, which some may find

129

intimidating, though relief soon comes, a second viewpoint being reached. From here Pico Ruivo, obscured by Pico das Torres from the first viewpoint, can be seen.

Now descend steeply, with sections of engineered steps, going through a rock arch and on to a tunnel which burrows through the Pico do Gato, the needle-like Cat's Peak. Beyond the tunnel bear left, soon reaching four more tunnels in quick succession. Beyond the last tunnel the path is easier, there even being a few windswept trees to soften the scenery: continue to the café below the summit of Pico Ruivo, perhaps stopping for a drink after visiting the high point.

To continue to Achada do Teixeira, follow the engineered path heading down from the café. To return to Pico de Arieiro, reverse the outward route.

3. Rabaçal

Although the drive to Rabaçal is hair-raising, from the road's end there are two short walks through some of the island's prettiest country.

Start/Finish

Rabaçal, reached by car or taxi from Funchal.

Distance/Ascent

The **Waterfall Walk** is about 1.5km (1 mile), the **25 Springs Walk** is about 5km (3 miles). Neither walk involves any significant climbing.

Time

Waterfall Walk, about 30 minutes. 25 Springs Walk about 1^1/$_2$ hours.

Difficulties

None, both walks are gentle though there is one exposed section on the longer walk.

From the car park at the end of the road, bear right, down steps, soon reaching the *Levada* do Risco. The *levada* is one of the prettiest on Madeira, with banks of moss and overhanging trees. Follow it for a couple of minutes to reach a track coming in from the right. Remember this junction as it is easy to go wrong on the return. Bear left and, after a few more minutes, you will reach a clear path (unsigned on my last visit) to the left, which descends to the Vinte e Cinco Fontes (25 Springs).

To reach the waterfall, continue along *Levada* do Risco to reach a fork where the *levada* goes right (needing a few steps up to a concrete path), while a path goes left. Bear right, soon reaching a viewpoint of the waterfall. At the time of writing there is a collapsed section close to the viewpoint, though this can be easily crossed if care is taken. At present the tunnel behind the falls is prohibited to walkers, the authorities considering its use dangerous,. If it is open and you are tempted to reach the viewpoint beyond, be prepared for a soaking, taking care of cameras and videos. The tunnel, and the ground beyond, is also very slippery: please take great care. To return, reverse the outward route.

The 25 Springs Walk descends from the first fork, using steps to reach the *Levada* das 25 Fontes. Turn right - the Risco waterfall is visible from here - and continue to reach the Ribiera Grande which is crossed to a curious well-head spring building. Now be cautious, the *levada* is narrow and the drop into the gorge on the left is about 30m (100ft), though the water channel is a good safety rail. Beyond this difficult section, ignore a path going downhill to the left to reach (after a further 10 minutes or so) a path uphill to the right. Take this, soon reaching the 25 Springs, a hollow into which a number (but not 25) waterfalls tumble. To return, reverse the outward route.

4. Levada dos Tornos

A walk for garden lovers, linking Madeira's two finest gardens along a *levada* which is almost a linear garden.

Start
Quinta do Palheiro (Blandy's Garden). This can be reached by Horãrios do Funchal buses Nos. 29, 36 or 37.

Finish
Jardim Botânico, Funchal. Horãrios do Funchal bus 31 which runs regularly throughout the day.

Distance/Ascent
5km (3 miles), with limited climbing.

Time
1 1/2 hours.

Difficulties
None, though can be muddy and slippery after rain.

From the gateway to Blandy's Garden, turn right (assuming you were exiting after a visit), following the garden's wall uphill to reach a road junction by a café. Turn left, uphill, then left again at the top to walk beside the Ramazotti Warehouse, soon reaching the *Levada* dos Tornos. The *levada* is the most important one on the island, over 100km (more than 60 miles) long and completed only in 1966. The water it collects on the northern slopes of the island is channelled to a hydro-electric power station at Fajã de Nogueira and then on to the south coast.

Follow the *levada* easily, soon reaching a fine viewpoint on the left - it is actually the flat roof of a school! Cross Highway 102, from where there is a good view of Funchal, and continue along a less pleasant stretch of the *levada*. This soon ends, the *levada* entering pine woods dotted with mimosas before reaching Highway 201. Cross and continue along the *levada*, now walking through a beautiful section of fragrant eucalyptus woodland. Cross another road and go past a water-control station to reach the Quinta do Pomar.

Here we leave the *levada*, which continues north towards Romeiras, going behind the mansion and its lovely little chapel. Rejoin the *levada*, briefly, to reach the red door exit from the quinta. Turn left and follow a cobbled road steeply downhill. Where the road turns sharp left, go straight ahead along an equally steep (and also cobbled) path, soon regaining the road near a restaurant.

Turn right, then, soon, left along Caminho dos Voltas. Follow this downhill for about 10 minutes to reach the entrance to the Jardim Botânico.

131

5. Eira do Serrado to Curral

Few visitors to Madeira will want to miss the journey to Curral das Freiras. The view from the car park above the village is stunning: this walk follows the old route into the village from that viewpoint.

Start

Eira do Serrado. Horãrios do Funchal bus No. 81 runs from Funchal to Curral das Freiras, stopping at the viewpoint. The bus also stops on its return from Curral to Funchal. Buses run approximately hourly all day (but less frequently on Saturdays and Sundays).

Finish

Curral das Freiras. See comments on 'Start'

Distance/ Ascent

4.5km (3 miles) and a descent of about 500m (1,650ft)

Time

1^1/$_2$ hours.

Difficulties

None, though in places the ground crossed is uneven.

From the parking area follow the well-trodden path towards the viewpoint of the mountain cauldron in which Curral das Freiras sits. A visit to the viewpoint is a must, but is actually a detour, the route descending from the concrete pillar in the car park. Follow the cobbled path which descends through chestnut trees - these have recently been overpruned but are struggling to re-assert themselves. Soon, a marvellous view opens out, taking in the road, to the right, and the village below: the path has actually passed above the road tunnel, then performed a sharp left turn as the far tunnel entrance was approached. The path now bears away from the road: continue more steeply downhill around a series of bends. There are occasional rock falls here and they can make the going awkward, but the path improves again when terraces are reached. The church in Curral is now at the same level as the path, but there is still work to do: continue along the path to reach a road. Turn right and follow the road uphill into Curral.

6. Levada da Central da Ribeira da Janela

Remote from Funchal, and well off the beaten track, this walk along a new *levada* offers great views of some of Madeira's finest terracing as it heads towards the moorland of the island's north-west.

Start/Finish

The small reservoir in Lamaceiros, above Porto Moniz. This can be reached by car or taxi, by taking the road beside the church in Lamaceiros, then going ahead where this road turns very sharply right. There is parking where the *levada* reaches the reservoir.

Distance/Ascent

Any distance up to 10km (6.25 miles). Gentle ascents.

Time

Up to 2^1/$_2$ hours.

Difficulties

There are exposed sections, but anyone with a head for heights will find these acceptable.

The Madeira Tourist Office considers the walk from Paúl da Serra across the wilderness of Fanal and then along the *Levada* da Central to Ribeira da Janela to be one its Top Thirteen. But this is a 20km (12.5 mile) route and has two major drawbacks for the average walker: the *levada* (when it is reached) starts by going through eight tunnels, a total time underground of almost an hour, requiring not only torches but a willingness to get very wet. The *levada* also has very exposed sections which will test the nerve of those used to scrambling in mountain regions. The section of the *levada* we shall follow has its moments, but they are nothing in comparison. We shall therefore content ourselves with an out-and-back walk: any distance covered will be worthwhile, but reaching the first tunnel involves a round trip of 10km.

From the car park by the reservoir, follow the *levada* - another new channel, opened in 1965 - through a scented grove of apple and fig trees and a few fennel bushes (as close as most visitors to Funchal may get to the plant that named the city). Beyond the filtration plant (reached after about 30 minutes or so) the *levada* widens. All walkers should reach this point at least as there is a magnificent view into the valley of the Ribiera da Janela with its tightly-packed terraces.

The *levada* now threads away through more rugged country, with shady patches of ferns and rock outcrops, and an increasingly spectacular view ahead towards Paúl da Serra. Continue to the mouth of the first tunnel, reversing the route from there, with equally spectacular views towards the north-western tip of the island.

7. Levada da Serra do Faial

This *levada* can be followed along its entire 27km (17 miles) length from Choupana to Portela, but such a walk is a major undertaking and, given the Madeiran climate, beyond the capabilities of average walkers. It is therefore better to follow a section. Luckily buses serve a number of points along the route and it is possible to complete walks of 5-15km (3-9 miles). Below two walks are suggested.

Start

Águas Mansas. This hamlet lies on Highway 102 a little way north of Camacha and is on the route of Horãrios do Funchal bus No. 77 which leaves Funchal for Santo da Serra daily from 7.30am, leaving approximately every 2^1/$_2$ hours.

Finish

Shorter Walk - Sitio das Quatro Estradas, also on Highway 102 and served by Horãrios do Funchal bus No. 77 which returns from Santo da Serra to Funchal approximately every 2^1/$_2$ hours. **Longer Walk** - Santo da Serra. Horãrios do Funchal bus No. 77 returns to Funchal (as for shorter walk above). From Santo SAM bus No. 20 also returns to Funchal, via Machico and the coast road. This service is also at approximately 2^1/$_2$ hour intervals.

Time

Shorter Walk - 6km (4 miles), limited climbing early in the walk.
Longer Walk - 15km (9 miles), limited climbing, as above.

Difficulties

None, a very straightforward walk. It is popular with walk organisers on the island and so you could meet, or pass, large groups of walkers.

Águas Mansas is set where Highway 206 meets Highway 102. Continue along Highway 102 in the direction of Santo da Serra for about 100m to reach a track on the left. Take this, going uphill for about 800m to reach the *Levada* da Serra do Faial. Turn right along the *levada*, following it to Highway 202, a distance of about 4km (2.5 miles) sometimes through eucalyptus woodland, sometimes through more open country with gorse and rhododendrons.

At the road, the shorter walk turns right: walk down to Sítio das Quatro Estradas - the Place of Four Roads, an apt description as Highway 202 crosses Highway 102 here.

The longer walk crosses the road and continues along the *levada*. After about 5km (3 miles), through country as good as that on the first stage of the walk, you will reach a crossing track at the Santo waterhouse. Turn right and follow the track downhill for about 1.5km (1 mile) to reach Highway 102. Turn right, then, after about 500m, turn left to walk into Santo da Serra.

8. Santana to São Jorge

For strong walkers - one might perhaps say explorers - the ascent of Penha de Águia (Eagle's Rock) is the walk/climb on the north coast. But it is a difficult route, especially early in the season when the rampant vegetation has not been chopped back. This coastal walk is a fine alternative, linking two exquisite villages with excellent views throughout.

Start

Santana. The walk leaves Highway 101 near the Velho Solar, a ruined mansion about 1.5km (1 mile) north of the centre of Santana. If you are using this trip to explore the village, you will want to walk that section of road. If not, ask the bus driver for Velho Solar. The bus is São Roque do Faial Nos. 103 or 138. No. 103 has departures from Funchal at 7.15am and 1.30pm (there are also two later departures, but these are of no use to walkers), but only the earlier bus runs on Sundays. No. 138 has a useful service only at 11.30am, and this does not run on Sundays either.

Finish

São Jorge. The same buses return to Funchal, with departures timed to give walkers adequate time for the walk. Walkers with their own transport can, of course, use the bus merely to return to Santana.

Distance/Ascent

5km (3 miles) with about 400m (1,350ft) of climbing. But add 1.5km (1 mile) if starting from the centre of

Santana, and 2.5km (1.5 miles) if either of the suggested detours is walked.

Time

1 1/2 hours, with an extra 3/4 hour for each of the detours, and an extra 1/2 hour if starting from Santana.

From Santana, follow Highway 101 northwards towards São Jorge to reach the bus stop by the Velho Solar. Take the old cobbled road to the ruin, bearing right by it on to a cobbled path above the vineyards of Achada do Gramacho. At a metalled road (at Quinta do Furão) turn left for 10m, then turn right along a road which passes beneath the Cabeço da Vigia, a cone-like hill. Just before the high point of the road, turn left along a track which soon descends a series of picturesque hairpins, the apexes of alternate bends close to the cliff edge. The view of the coast is breathtaking, but is matched by that of the high peaks inland, to the left.

At the bottom of the hairpins, cross the bridge over the Ribeira de São Jorge and turn right along a path beside the sea, soon reaching all that now remains of the old port of Calhau. As the ruins are reached there is a path on the left. This is the way to Sao Jorge, but a short detour is worthwhile, following the coast path to a deep-cut inlet below the lighthouse which sits above the Ponta de São Jorge. There is a bridge here, but it is of dubious quality. Admire the view from this side and then return to Calhau.

Follow the path from the ruin steeply uphill (with a terrific view of the hairpin path you descended) to reach a road. Cross and bear slightly left to go up steps to São Jorge cemetery. Turn right along the road, passing a chapel to reach a junction. Turn left to reach the church and bus stop in São Jorge.

For a second worthwhile detour, return to the chapel passed on the approach to São Jorge and turn left to follow Estrada Municipal do Farrobo. At a T-junction, turn right to reach the Faro de São Jorge, the lighthouse seen on the earlier detour. From it there are wonderful views of the coast. Reverse the route to return to São Jorge.

9. Pico Ruivo to Encumeada

The traverse from Pico Areiero to Pico Ruivo is the peak-baggers walk. This longer route is for the mountain connoisseur. A magnificent walk, but not one to be undertaken lightly as it is more remote and weatherswept.

Start

Achada do Teixeira. This can be reached by taxi from Santana. If you are staying at Funchal it is best to travel to Santana the right before the walk, otherwise the best of the day (and probably the best of the weather) will be spent travelling.

Finish

Boca da Encumeada. The pass between the north coast (São Vicente) and the south (Ribeira Brava) is crossed by two buses, only one of which is useful. Rodoeste bus No. 139 from Santa/Porto Moniz operates on Monday, Wednesday and Friday only and reaches Encumeada at 6.40am(!), continuing to Funchal which it reaches at 8.30am. For walkers heading east (towards the

135

rising sun) a No. 139 leaves Funchal at 9am, arriving at Encumeada at 10.55am.

The better bus is Rodoeste No. 6. There are three daily each way from Funchal to Boaventura. The first Funchal bus, at 7.35am reaches Encumeada at 9.30am for those wanting to walk towards the sun. Those who want it on their backs (as described) will find only one bus useful (as the first two reach Encumeada at 7.05am and 8.25am). This leaves Encumeada at 4.10pm, arriving Funchal at 5.50pm.

Distance
15km (9.5 miles) with around 600m (2,000ft) of ascent and rather Ascent: more descent.

Time
4½ hours.

Difficulties
There is only one bus per day - miss it at your peril! The walking is straightforward, but the route is remote and low cloud - which is very possible - can make route following tricky at times. Please be prepared for rain and cold winds, and carry supplies of water and food.

From Achada do Teixeira - most notable for the curious basaltic natural sculpture known as the Homem em Pé, the Man on Foot, which might remind British walkers of Dartmoor's tors - follow the engineered path towards the summit of Pico Ruivo, passing the path from Pico Arieiro (on the left) and the café/resthouse to reach a sign suggesting it is 16km to Encumeada. This seems unduly pessimistic: ignore the information, and the steps up to Pico Ruivo's summit, but follow the sign. There are a few paint splashes on the rocks ahead, but the path is largely unmarked, though obvious, as it heads west towards the Torrinhas Pass.

The walking to the Pass is magnificent, with stunning views, particularly south towards Curral das Freiras. Ignore all paths which head that way, and all those which head north. Your route is almost due west, and is also well-trodden. Just before the Torrinhas Pass, and about 2½ hours from the start, another path heading down to Curral is reached: bear right to reach a precarious descent down smooth steps with no guard-rail and an impressive drop. Be cautious here. Beyond, steep steps climb to the Torrinhas Pass.

At the pass there is a signpost, but the way is clear, involving a long climb to the top of Pico do Jorge. At the base of the descent from the peak there is a refreshing spring and a picturesque rock arch. The route now descends through a fern-ladened, shady gorge formed of cliffs of basalt to reach a large patch of folhados (lily trees) and the top of an almost continuous series of steps leading down towards Encumeada. The steps finish at a track which is followed to the main road at the pass.

10. Levada do Caldeirão Verde

Though exposed almost throughout, this fine walk is well protected and should be within the capabilities of most walkers. A torch is essential for the tunnelled sections.

Start/Finish

Queimadas. Walkers with their own transport will be able to drive to the start. Others should take a taxi from Santana.

Distance/Ascent

13km (8 miles) for the round trip, with a climb of about 200m (650ft).

Time

3 1/2 hours.

Difficulties

The walk is very straightforward, but in addition to the exposure it can also be very slippery. Slippery conditions and big drops are not a happy combination, so please be careful. As mentioned above, a torch is essential for the tunnelled section.

From Queimadas, go past the guesthouses, cross an old bridge and follow the wide, but slippery, path beside the *Levada* do Caldeirão Verde. Soon the walker must leave the *levada* briefly as the path has fallen away, but the water channel is soon rejoined and followed across the gorges of two rivers, the Ribeira dos Cedros (after about 2km - 1.25 miles) and the Ribeira do Fonte do Louro (after about 3.5 km - 2.5 miles). Soon after the second gorge you will reach a tunnel. This tunnel is short, but just beyond it (and a path to the right for the Vale da Lapa) a longer one is reached. A third tunnel - with limited headroom: be careful - follows, beyond which the path leaves the *levada* briefly, then goes through a fourth, and final tunnel.

Continue beside the *levada* for another 10 minutes or so to reach a spillway. Climb the path to the left of this to reach the Caldeirão Verde, the Green Cauldron, a truly lovely spot where a tall waterfall (almost 300m - 1,000 ft) drops into a glistening pool. To return to Queimadas, reverse the outward route from here.

A worthwhile extension of this walk is possible for very experienced walkers. The route is very exposed and prone to landslides and should not be undertaken by anyone who is not both agile and absolutely sure-footed above big drops. The extension - of about 4km (2.5 miles) there and back, taking at least 1.25 hours - continues along the *levada* for about 15 minutes, then goes up steps (exposed, especially on the descent) to reach the *Levada* do Pico Ruivo. This almost immediately enters a tunnel (which is almost 2.5km - 1.5 miles - long): bear right by the water tank, go under a waterfall (a guaranteed shower) and through four short tunnels to reach the gorge of the Ribeira Grande. Cross two precarious-looking bridges and go through a further four short tunnels to reach the Caldeirão do Inferno, the Cauldron of Hell, a wild, beautiful spot. The route must be reversed to return to Queimadas.

11. Ribeiro Frio: Levada do Furado

A short walk making the most of the lovely country around Ribeiro Frio. There is one exposed section, but even those who turn around there will have enjoyed a wonderful walk.

Start/Finish

Ribeiro Frio. Walkers with their own transport can park in the hamlet where there is parking across from the restaurant. Ribeiro Frio is on the route of three buses of São Roque do Faial, Nos. 56, 103 and 138, though only the latter two have departure times that are likely to appeal to the walker.

Distance/Ascent

7kms (4.5 miles) with limited climbing. A walk to the exposed section is a round trip of about 3kms (2 miles).

Time

1 3/4 hours, the walk to the exposed section requiring about 45 minutes.

Just below the restaurant in Ribeiro Frio (heading towards Faial) is a sign, on the right, for Portela. Take this delightful path descending steps to a waterfall, on the right, and then continuing beside the *Levada* do Furado. Follow the water channel to the exposed section, the big drop being on the left. The return from here will give walkers - especially those new to Madeira's *levada* walking - a good introduction to the routes, and also some delightful views.

Beyond the exposed section of path, go past a waterfall and continue in straightforward fashion, with superb views down into the valley of the Ribeiro Frio and also west towards Portela. The *levada* turns south, executes a leftward curve and then bears back right to reach a bridge over the Ribeiro Bezerro. This is the end of the walk - though the path continues to Portela, about 2 1/2 hours walking away. The grassed area by the bridge is a popular picnic site. With two waterfalls feeding the *levada*, and the river itself, it is marvellously picturesque.

To return, reverse the outward route, taking care on the exposed section.

12. Bica da Cana: Levada do Serra

A short walk with magnificent views of the high peaks and the north coast. The objective is a basalt boss known as Pináculo, the Pinnacle.

Start/Finish

The viewpoint of Bica da Cana on the eastern edge of Paúl da Serra. Walkers with their own transport can reach this easily.

Other walkers will need to use a taxi as there are no buses to this point.

Distance/Ascent

5km (3 miles), with about 150m (500 ft) of climbing.

Time

1 1/2 hours.

Difficulties

None.

The walk starts at the red and white pillars at the entrance to the Bica da Cana Refuge. Follow the clear path through the ferns - there are likely to be other walkers on the route, especially at the weekend - to reach a stone marker with an arrow directing you to the top of the peak. This is a detour, but is worthwhile as from the triangulation point you can see the entire route as well as enjoying a view of the high Madeiran peaks which form a jagged line on the horizon.

Follow the path to reach the source of the *Levada* da Serra and turn right with it, following it past the obvious, green-clad pinnacle. Beyond the pinnacle the *levada* starts to descend towards Encumeada. Turn back at any con-

138

venient point, reversing the outward route to rejoin the start. If you have not visited the triangulation point on the outward journey, climb up to it now, bearing left, uphill, to reach a fence. There are stiles over this fence: walk towards the peak, following a rugged, but short, path (which involves a short scramble) on the left to reach the actual summit. From the top go downhill to rejoin the outward route, or head directly towards the road, crossing a couple of stiles then turning right along the road to regain the start.

Guided Walks

Those visitors who wish to explore Madeira on foot, but would prefer to do so with a knowledgeable guide should contact the Tourist Office in Funchal who will be able to put them in touch with organisations who offer day and multi-day walk programmes. Two organisations who offer walking holidays are:

Eurofun

Navio Azul Shopping Centre
Estrada Monumental
9000 Funchal
Tel: 228638
Fax: 228620

Terras de Aventura & Turismo

Caminho do Amparo, 25
9000 Funchal
Tel/Fax: 61018

Banks, Credit Cards and Currency

Being part of Portugal, Madeira's currency is the euro.
All major credit cards are taken in most hotels, shops and restaurants, especially in Funchal. In more remote villages it is likely that cash only will be accepted. Many hotels, restaurants and shops in Funchal also accept travellers cheques.
Banks are open from 8.30am-3pm Monday to Friday. In Funchal some of the larger banks also open on Saturday mornings (9am-1pm). There are also Bureau de Change which open 9am-1pm and 2-7pm Monday to Friday and 9am-7pm on Saturdays.

Camping

Madeira has only one official camp site, the Parque de Campismo at Porto Moniz, Tel: 853872. However, semi-official camp sites, with taps and barbecue facilities exist at several places, chiefly in the forests.
There is also an official camp site on Porto Santo – Parque de Campismo on Rua Goulart Madeiros, Vila Baleira, Tel: 983111.

Children

It has to be admitted that Madeira does not have an extensive array of attractions specifically for children. However, what there is will keep younger children happy, while for older, more adventurous children there is plenty to keep them occupied.
For younger children, many of the bigger hotels have play areas and swimming pools. Elsewhere the following are excellent:

Aquapark
Santa Cruz
Tel 524412
Open: All year, daily 10am-7.30pm (7pm September-March)
A fine collection of slides, flumes and pools.

Parque Temático
Santana
Tel:
Open: All year, daily 10am-7pm (6pm September-March)
A collection of buildings housing multi-media shows on various aspects of Madeiran life, past, present and future. Not as dull as it sounds, though doing one after the other could be a bit too much. Outside there are playgrounds, a boating lake, miniature train and some more cultural things such as buildings in local style, craft workshops.

The Vulcanology centre at Grutas Centro de Vulcanismo and the Aquarium and Science Centre in Porto Moniz are definitely worth visiting. The Monte toboggans will amuse and excite, while boat trips from Funchal harbour are an exciting way of passing several hours. Some companies offer trips to watch the dolphins which frequent Madeira's coast. Of these, try:

Sea Born (Catamaran trips)
Tel: 231312

Ventura do Mar (Yacht trips)
Tel: 280033

Gavilão (Yacht trips)
Tel: 241124

For older, more adventurous children the suggestions below for canyoning, climbing, paragliding and water sports, are likely to appeal.

Climate

Average Daytime Maximum Temperatures

Month	°C	°F
January	18	65
February	19	67
March	19	67
April	20	68
May	21	70
June	22	72
July	24	75
August	25	77
September	25	77
October	24	75
November	22	72
December	20	68

The average sea temperature in summer is about 21°C (70°F) with a maximum in August. It falls to about 16°C (60°F) in winter.

Number of Days of Rain (in Funchal)

Month	Days of Rain	Rainfall	mm
January	7	100	4.0
February	6	90	3.5
March	7	75	3.0
April	4	45	1.8
May	2	25	1.0
June	1	10	0.4
July	0	0	0
August	1	5	0.2
September	2	30	1.2
October	7	75	3.0
November	7	100	4.0
December	7	75	3.0

The above should not be taken too literally as Madeira's mountains create a micro-climate which produce rain more frequently on the tops and also on the north coast. Much of the rain also falls as sharp showers.

Restaurants

Western Madeira

Moderate

Marisqueiria Rocha Mar
Calheta
Tel: 823600
Excellent sea food and in a position which allows envious glances over the expensive boats in harbour.

Orca
Porto do Muniz
Tel: 850000
Very popular, and rightly so. Good menu and excellent cooking.

Solar do Pero
Ponta do Pargo
Tel: 882170
A combination of snack bar and restaurant, so good for a quick lunch or a very good evening meal.

Inexpensive

Borda d'Agua
Ribeira Brava
No telephone
Good position, particularly when the sea is rough and the windows are closed. Inexpensive, but excellent.

Cachalote
Porto Moniz
Tel: 853150
Simple, but very pleasant.

Onda Azul
Calheta
Tel: 820300
Nicely positioned and with a very good menu.

Central Madeira

Expensive

Eira do Serrado
Tel; 710060
The only place in town. Not too expensive, but the little extra is worth it for the stunning views over the Curral des Freiras. Traditional Madeiran dishes.

Pousada de Pico do Arieiro
Tel: 230110
The restaurant of the guesthouse set on top of Madeira's third highest peak. Good food and very pleasant surroundings. The restaurant by the car park is cheaper but also worthwhile.

Moderate

Churchill's Place
Câmara de Lobos
Tel: 944336
As close as you can get to where the great man set up his easel. He would probably have approved of the menu too.

O Colmo
Santana
Tel: 572478
Good Madeiran cooking in the restaurant close to the more touristy of the village palheiros.

Ribeiro Frio (formerly Victor's)
Tel: 575898
Trout is the speciality - as though you needed to be told!

Inexpensive

Encumeada
Encumeada Pass
Tel: 951281

The restaurant of the guesthouse. Perhaps more 'moderate' than 'inexpensive', but well worth the extra for the good helpings of warming traditional food.

O Virgilio
São Vicente
Tel: 842467
With its log fire – which doubles up as a cooking stove – this is rather more than the snack bar it first appears.

Ribamar
Câmara de Lobos
Tel: 944336
Beautifully set fish restaurant, overlooking the sea. It is no surprise to find it specialises in fish dishes

Eastern Madeira

Expensive

La Perla
Qunita Splendida
Tel: 930400
In the mansion at the heart of the gardens. One of the island's finest restaurants with interesting dishes on a vaguely Italian theme. Try the beef served on hot volcanic stone.

Vista Mar
Garajau
Tel: 934110
Aimed at the tourist market (though none the worse for that), but has some surprising items on the menu.

Moderate

Café Relógio
Camacha
Tel: 922114
Almost a compulsory visit for the wickerwork shop, but a good menu and lovely views while you are eating.

Mercado Velho
Rua do Mercado
Machico
Tel: 965926
Very atmospheric position and building. Good cooking as well.

Inexpensive

Franco
Sítio da Queimada de Baixo
Machico
More a snack bar than a restaurant - just the place for a bite at lunchtime.

Tourigalo
Garajau
No telephone
Neat little place in the main street. Unpretentious and delightful.

Restaurants in Funchal

Expensive

Dona Amélia
Rua Imperatriz Donna Amélia, 83
Tel: 225784
Arguably the best place in town, quality international cooking, with prices to match. Housed in elegant nineteenth century mansion. Close to the Casino complex.

Casa Madeirense
Estrada Monumental, 153
Tel: 766700
Very good Madeiran cooking with a few chef's specials. Very atmospheric.

Casa Velha
Rua Imperatriz Dona Amélia, 69
Tel: 225749
Another converted nineteenth century mansion close to the Casino complex. Some Madeiran cooking, but a few interesting alternatives - try the lobster and pasta.

Quinta Magnólia
Rua do Dr Pita
Tel: 764013
Home of the Madeiran chef's school - good food and occasionally challenging combinations. Only open for lunch.

Quinta Palmeira
Avenida do Infante, 5
Tel: 221814
Between the Casino and the Savoy hotel. Very elegant, especially on the terrace. Excellent menu and cooking.

Moderate

Mar Azul
Marina
Tel: 230563
Very good chicken and fish dishes in a style as traditional as the waitress' uniforms.

Arsénio's
Rua de Santa Maria, 169
Tel: 224007
Popular for the nightly fado singing, but equally good for its traditional food.

Tappassol
Rua Dom Carlos I, 62
Tel: 225023
Extraordinary menu which includes authentic espada with banana and such things as octopus stew. Rooftop terrace to add to the romance.

The Vagrant
Avenida do Mar
Tel: 223572
The old Beatles boat, now set in unmovable (and so seasickness free) concrete. More for the atmosphere than the food, but good Madeiran cooking and excellent pizzas.

Inexpensive

Marisa
Rua de Santa Maria, 162
Tel: 226189
Small, quiet family run restaurant with excellent Madeiran cooking. Try the caldeirada.

O Jango
Rua de Santa Maria, 166
Tel: 211280
Tiny place - booking required to be certain of a seat - with excellent cooking. The paella is well worth a try.

Café Esplanade Arco-Velho
Rua de Carlos I, 42
Don't be deceived, this is more than a bar. Good Madeiran dishes in no-nonsense setting.

Paladar
Rua das Hortas, 31
Tel: 220503
Very good for lunch - just watch how many locals go there - but also worth a try in the evenings.

Nightlife

Funchal

Funchal is a quiet, pleasant city, the perfect centre for a relaxing holiday spent touring the scenic delights of Madeira. But at night it becomes a livelier place, with something for everyone:

Discotecas

The best are, of course, a matter of opinion, but the following are usually numbered among the better ones.

Girassol, Hotel Girassol, Estrada Monumental

Vespas, 7 Avenida Francisco Sá Carneiro

Mar, Hotel Do Mar, Estrada Monumental

O Farol, Hotel Madeira Carlton, Largo António Nobre

O Molhe, Forte de Nossa Senhora da Conceição, Estrada da Pontinha
Housed in the fortress that once protected Funchal's harbour.

Formula 1, Rua do Favilha 5

Nightclubs

The best - those with a good floor show - are in the big hotels, but a couple in the main are also worth trying:
Pestana Casino Park Hotel

Madeira Carlton Hotel

Galâxia, at the Savoy Hotel

O Fugitivo, 66a Rua Imperatriz Dona Amélia

Bars

This really depends on what the visitor is seeking. For something local in character, try:

Berlights, on the corner of Estrada Monumental and Rua do Gorgulho

Number Two, Rua do Favilha

The places with the best fado singing are

Arsénio's, 169 Rua de Santa Maria

Marcelino, 22 Travessa das Torres

Theatre/Music/Cinema

For a quieter evening, look for the programme at the Municipal Theatre in Avenida Arriaga, though concerts and other productions are somewhat few in number.

Films are shown at the multi-screen Cinemax in the Marina Shopping Centre in Avenida Arriaga, the Lusomondo in the Forum Shopping Centre at the west end of the hotel 'zone' and the Castello Lopez in the Madeira Shopping Centre in São Martinho a north-western suburb of the city. Many of the films shown are new releases in English (with Portuguese sub-titles). Films are also occasionally shown in the Municipal Theatre.

Casino

For a much more serious evening with the chance to lose a lot of money the Casino de Madeira can be found in the Casino complex. It is open from 5pm to 3am, you will need to show your passport to gain entrance, you must be over 21 years of age, and smart clothing (men in jacket and tie, ladies in dresses, though smart trouser suits will probably be admitted) must be worn.

Shops

Shops are normally open 9am-1pm and 3-7pm Monday to Friday and 9am-1pm on Saturdays. The Funchal shopping centres are open daily 10am-10pm. Many tourist shops are also open longer hours and at weekends.

Shopping in Funchal

The Marina Shopping Centre, the shopping mall near the harbour, is the easiest place to get most things the visitor might require, but though well designed and equally well organised it is a little soul-less in comparison to other parts of the city. Other, newer centres have made the shopping experience a bit more pleasurable. At the western end of the hotel 'zone' – and reached by special buses – the Forum Madeira has around 80 shops and several good cafes. Special buses also reach Madeira shopping in the north-west suburb of São Martinho where there are over 100 shops, together with cafes, restaurants, a bowling alley and cinema. Within the hotel 'zone' is the Lido/Eden Mar centre with a more limited selection of shops.

The area with the greatest character is that near the cathedral where the little alleys are home to all sorts of unlikely shops. Equally good is the 'market' area of Rua do Aljube, also close to the cathedral, the Bazar de Povo which extends to the bridge over the Ribeira da Santa Luzia, and Rua Fernão de Ornelas.
The designer outlets tend to be in Rua das Pretas and Rua dos Ferreiros, near the cathedral.
Shops selling souvenirs are everywhere. To get a good overall view of Madeira handicrafts visit the Casa do Turista in Rua do Conseilheiro. This may not be the best place to buy though. For wickerwork you should go to Camacha, for embroidery to the 'factory' outlet of Patricio and Gouveia at 33 Rua do Visconde de Anadia which runs parallel to the Ribeira de Santa Luzia or to the IBTAM showroom/museum. For flowers visit the flower sellers near the cathedral or the Mercado dos Lavradores. The stalls near the Mercado are also excellent for the traditional Madeiran footwear, the leather botas. For wine, there is a multitude of choice, but the São Francisco wine lodge should be visited before buying anything.

Consulates

British
2-4 Avenida Zarco, Funchal, Tel: 221221
(Commonwealth citizens are also welcome here)

USA
4th Floor, Apartamento B, Edificio Infante Bloco B, Avenida Luis de Comões, Funchal, Tel: 235636

Customs and Entry Regulations

Technically visitors from the European Union require only some form of identification, but it is recommended that a full passport is carried. Visitors from the US, Canada, Australia and New Zealand are issued with a 60-day tourist visa on arrival.
The customs limits from Madeira to Britain are as for all other countries of the European Union. Visitors from other countries should check their limits before buying. There are several Tax Free shops on the island which remove Portuguese VAT from purchases.

Disabled Visitors

Sadly there are few facilities for disabled visitors other than those offered by the airport and the more expensive hotels.

Electricity

220v 50Hz with a continental-style two-pin socket.

Emergencies

For Police, Fire or Ambulance Tel: 112

There are 24-hour casualty services at:
Hospital Cruz de Carvalho, Avenida Luis Camões, Tel: 705600

There is an emergency dental service at:
Clinica Dentária Cinco de Outubro, 79a Rua 5 de Outubro, Tel: 7950143

Health Care

Visitors from Britain should obtain an European Health Insurance Form (EHIC) from a Post Office (or online at www.dh.gov.uk/travellers or from the EHIC Application Line on 0845 6062030. As a member of the European Union, Portugal has reciprocal health arrangements. Some visitors may feel that taking out travel insurance, not only as a protection against loss or theft but which includes such health extras as repatriation in the event of major illnesses or accidents is worthwhile.
Visitors from countries outside the European Union should check their own health insurance.
There are three hospitals in Funchal and a number of health centres throughout the island.
The water is safe to drink, but bottled water is widely available.

Language

The official language of Madeira is Portuguese, but English is widely spoken in towns and villages most frequented by visitors.

National Holidays

Madeira celebrates Portuguese national holidays:

1 January

25 April - Revolution Day

1 May

10 June - Camões Day

1 July - Day of Discovery of Madeira

15 August - Festival of Assumption

5 October - Republic Day

1 November - All Saints' Day

1 December - Restoration Day

8 December - Immaculate Conception

25 December

In addition there are several regional and religious holidays.

Newspapers

The main Madeiran daily newspaper, the Diário de Notícias produces a supplement in English which is delivered to the main hotels. The supplement covers international and local news and includes the day's weather forecast and TV programmes.
The monthly Agenda Cultural is also in English. It, too, is available at the larger hotels and also from the Tourist Information Offices.

Pharmacies

A Farmácia displays a white cross on a green background. They are open normal shop hours, but all indicate the pharmacy which is open on the 24-hour rota. During shop hours English-speakers should go to the Botica Inglesa, 23-25 Rua Câmara Pestana, Funchal, Tel: 220158

Post and Telephone Services

Post Offices are Correios. The main one in Funchal is close to Zarco's statue in Avenida Zarco. The staff there speak reasonable English. At most post offices you may also make phone calls from special booths, paying for the call once you have finished. Post offices keep shop hours, but the telephone booths stay open longer, usually until 10pm.
Normal telephones use telephone cards obtainable from post offices or shops showing a Credifone sign. The code for an international call is 00. The country codes are:

UK	(00) 44
Eire	(00) 353
Canada	(00) 1
USA	(00) 1
Australia	(00) 61
New Zealand	(00) 64

When calling abroad remember to drop the first '0' of the number you ring, ie. to call the Portuguese Tourist Office in London from Madeira dial 00-44-20-7494-5720.

Sport

Canoeing and Kayaking

Experts will find Madeira's rivers and coastal waters offer as much excitement as they can handle. Beginners are less well catered for, but some of the Madeiran clubs will help. In either case, contact:

Clube Naval do Funchal
São Lázaro, Marina do Funchal
Tel: 224661

Clube Naval do Porto Santo
Vila Baleira
Tel: 982085

Terras de Aventura
Caminho do Amparo, 25
Funchal
Tel: 776818

Canyoning and Rock Climbing

Terras de Aventura
Caminho do Amparo, 25
Funchal
Tel: 776818

Diving

The deep, but warm, waters off Madeira are excellent for diving, the volcanic nature of the island being a complete contrast to normal dive waters. Contact:

Baleia Diving Centre
Hotel Dom Pedro Baia
Machico
Tel: 052543

Baleira Diving
Hotel Vila Baleira
Porto Santo
Tel: 240548

Club de Mergulho
Hotel Don Pedro Garaju
Caniço
Tel: 934421

GaloDiving
Hotel Galamar
Caniço
Tel: 930939

Porto Santo Sub
Clube Naval do Porto Santo
Porto de Abrigo do Porto Santo
Tel: 916 033997

Scorpio Divers
Complexo Balnear do Lido
Funchal
Tel: 766977

Terras de Aventura
Caminho do Amparo, 25
Funchal
Tel: 776818

Tubarão Madeira-Mergulho
Rua do Vale das Neves, 73
Funchal
Tel: 794124

Game Fishing

Those wanting to try their hand at fishing for big fish out on the Atlantic should contact:

Albatroz do Mar
Marina do Funchal
Tel: 963 003864

Euromar
Avenida do Infante 58
Funchal
Tel: 200750

Fish Madeira
Travessa das Virtudes 123
Tel: 752685

Madeira Big Game Fishing
Rua Aspirante Mota Freitas 8
Funchal
Tel: 231823

Nautisantos
Marina da Funchal
Tel: 919 181510

Turipesca
Marina do Funchal
Tel: 231063
Tel: 231063

Golf

There are two courses, both of which are 18-hole:

Campo de Golfe da Madeira
San António da Serra
Tel: 550100

Sociedade Turística Palheiro Golfe
Sítio do Balançal
São Gonçalo, Funchal
Tel: 790120

Mini-golf is available at:

Quinta Magnólia
Funchal
Tel: 764598

Hang Gliding and Paragliding

Aeroclub da Madeira
Rua do Castanheiro
Funchal
Tel: 228311

Terras de Aventura
Caminho do Amparo, 25
Funchal
Tel: 776818

Horse Riding

There is one school on Madeira and another on Porto Santo:

Associação Hipicá da Madeira
Quinta Vale Pires, Caminho dos Pretos
Funchal
Tel: 792582

Centro Hipico do Porto Santo
Quinta dos Profetas
Porto Santo
Tel: 983165

Explorations by horse are also available, contact:

Club Ipismo
Quinta Vale Pires,
Caminho dos Pretos
Soã João Latrão
(on the ER201 road towards Terreiro da Luta from Monte)
Tel: 792582

Hipicentre
Sitio da Ponta
Porto Santo
Tel: 967 671689

Terras de Aventura
Caminho do Amparo, 25
Funchal
Tel: 776818

Squash
Public courts are available at:
Galomar Squash Centre, Tel: 934566
Pavilhão dos Trabalhadores, Tel: 763939

Quinta Magnólia
Rua do Dr Pita
Funchal
Tel: 764598

Swimming
Most of the bigger hotels have swimming pools. There is also an Olympic-size pool at the Municipal Lido, Rua do Gorgulho, Funchal. The lido is open daily from 8.30am-7pm (9am-6pm from October to March).

Tennis
Public courts are available at:
Associação de Ténis da Madeira, Tel: 228086
Clube de Ténis do Funchal, Tel: 763237
Quinta Magnólia, Tel: 764598
Rua do Dr Pita, Funchal, Tel: 764598

Water Sports
As might be expected, Madeira's waters offer marvellous sport.

For jet skiing contact:

Terras de Aventura
Caminho do Amparo, 25
Funchal
Tel: 776818

Urs Moser Diving Centre
Rua João Gonçalves Zarco
Porto Santo
Tel: 982162

For sailing contact:

Associação Regional de Vela, Remo e Canoagem
São Lázaro
Marina do Funchal
Tel: 224970

Centro de Treino Mar da Madeira
São Lázaro
Marina do Funchal
Tel: 224661

Clube Naval do Funchal
Marina do Funchal
Tel: 224661

Clube Naval do Porto Santo
Vila Baleira
Tel: 982085

For waterskiing contact:

Terras de Aventura
Caminho do Amparo, 25
Funchal
Tel: 776818

For windsurfing contact:

Clube Naval do Funchal
São Lázaro, Marina do Funchal
Tel: 224661

Complexo Balnear do Lido
Rua do Gorgulho
Funchal
Tel: 762217

Desportos Aquáticos do Porto Santo
Tel: 982035

Terras de Aventura
Caminho do Amparo, 25
Funchal
Tel: 776818

Time

From the last Sunday in March to the last Sunday in October Madeira is GMT + 1. During the winter the island is as GMT.

Tipping

Hotels and most restaurants add a service charge. Where this is not so, and for taxi drivers and guides 10% is considered correct. The Monte basket men deserve an extra 10% or so too if they have posed for pictures and given a particularly good ride.

Tourist Information Offices

Outside Madeira

GB
Portuguese National Tourist Office
c/o Portuguese Embassy
11 Belgrave Square
London
SW1X 8PP 3EJ
Tel: 020-7201-6666
Fax: 020-7201-6633

Canada
Portuguese National Tourist Office
60 Bloor Street West, Suite 1005
Toronto
Ontario
M4W 3B8
Tel: 416-921-7376
Fax: 416-921-1353

USA

Portuguese National Tourist Office
4th Floor
590 Fifth Avenue
New York 10036-4702
Tel: 646-723-0200/646-723-0299
Fax: 212-764-6137

Within Madeira

The telephone code for Portugal is 351, that for Madeira is 91 (091 from mainland Portugal)

The main office (Posto de Turismo) is at:

Avenida Arriaga, 18
9000 Funchal
Tel: 211900
Fax: 232151
It is open daily Monday-Friday 9am-8pm, Saturday 9am-6pm

Other offices (open Monday-Friday 9am-12noon and 2-5pm) are:

Câmara Municipal
Largo da República
9300 Câmara de Lobos
Tel: 942108

Forte Nossa Senhora do Amparo
9200 Machico
Tel: 962289

Vila do Porto Moniz
9270 Porto Moniz
Tel: 852555

Avenida Henrique Vieira e Castro
Vila Baleira
9400 Porto Santo
Tel: 982361

Forte de São Bento
9350 Ribeira Brava
Tel: 951675

Santa Caterina de Baixo (Airport)
9100 Santa Cruz
Tel: 524933
Only open to meet incoming flights.

Sitio do Serrado
9230 Santana
Tel: 572992

There is also an office at Porto Santo airport which is open only to coincide with incoming flights.

Travel

Getting to Madeira

For air travellers not arriving on a charter flight, the choice is now less limited than it was until very recently when TAP, the Portuguese national airline, had a monopoly of flights to Madeira. Several other European airlines are now operating flights, including British Airways. The TAP flights are still very attractive as they will allow a stop-over in Lisbon at no extra cost and occasionally have deals which include very cheap car hire.

From the airport there are buses to Funchal, but the taxi fare is very reasonable.

For those preferring to arrive by sea the situation is even worse as there are no ferry services to the island. Cruise ships do stop there, but trying to find a berth on one of these could be difficult.

Getting around Madeira

Buses are a reasonable way to travel around the island, especially if you want to admire the view or want to walk the levadas (see the chapter on Walking on Madeira). Various weekly and multi-day tickets are available. For details of these and of the bus timetable, visit the Tourist Information Office in Funchal.

Taxis are relatively cheap and are a useful idea for short journeys. If you are planning longer trips discuss the price beforehand. If you are using a taxi to reach the start of a walk and wish to be picked up at another point when you finish make sure that the price and time are well understood by both parties before you set out. Official taxis are black with green or cream roofs.

Car hire is not as cheap as might be expected, but does offer great freedom in terms of touring. All major car hire and several local ones have offices at the airport and in Funchal. You will need your national driving licence, but an international driving permit is not required. Drivers must be over 23 years of age. If you do hire a car please take great care, particularly on the north coast road and the in the mountains: the roads are narrow, often have unprotected edges and long, steep drops, and are prone to rockfalls.

Remember that you drive on the right in Madeira. The wearing of seat belts is compulsory and children under the age of 12 years are not allowed in front seats. The speed limits are 40kph (25mph) in town, 80kph (50mph) on roads out of town, and 110kph (68mph) on the expressway. Except for the centre of Funchal, parking is never much of a problem.

Index

A

Achada do Teixeira	85
Adegas de São Francisco	33
Alfândega	56
Arco da Calheta	78
Arco de São Jorge	86
Atlantic festival	14
Avenida Arriaga	33
Azulejos	36

B

Banks	140
Bertrand de Montluc	9,29
Bica da Cana	76,126
Bica da Cana: Levada do Serra	138
Boaventura	86
Boca do Encumeada	90
British Cemetery	45
Buses	125

C

Calheta	77
Camacha	107
Câmara de Lobos	92
Câmara Municipal	52
Campo de Baixo	115
Campo de Cima	115
Canhas	78
Caniçal	104
Capela da Senhora da Piedade	104
Capela de Corpo Santo	58
Capela de Santa Catarina	39
Capela de São Roque	101
Capela dos Milagres	101
Capela Nossa Senhora da Graça	117
Carnival of courtship	14
Carnival season	24
Casa de Colombo	114
Casa do Turista	37
Centro Museológico do Açucar	49
Chamber of Commerce	37
Chapel of Miracles	101
Chestnut Festival	25
Christopher Columbus	9,29,113
Church of Nossa Senhora da Piedade	114
Climate	141
Convento de Santa Clara	46
Convent of Santa Clara	38
Curral das Freiras	72
Currency	140

E

Eira do Serrado	72
Eira do Serrado to Curral	132
Encumeada	90,135
English Church	45
Equipment	124
Estreito da Calheta	78
Estreito da Câmara de Lobos	93
Eurofun	139

F

Faial	83,84
Festa do Campadres	24
Festa do Vinho	18
Festival of Bom Jesus	25
Festival of Nossa Senhora	24
Festival of Nossa Senhora da Piedade	25
Festival of Nossa Senhora de Rosario	25
Festival of Santissimo Sacramento	24
Festival of Sao Amaro	24
Festival of Senhora dos Milagres	25
Festival of the Assumption	24
Festivals of Santa Maria Madalena	24
Flemish	49
Flower festivals	24
Fortaleza da Sao João Batista	101
Fortaleza de Nossa Senhora do Amparo	101
Fortaleza de São Tiago	58
Fortaleza do Pico	46
Fortaleza São Lourenço	32
Funchal	26,80,83
Funchal Cathedral	48

G

Garajau	95

H

Henrique Alemão	81
Hospício da Princessa	41

I

IBTAM	59
Igreja (church) São Pedro	47
Igreja da Nossa Senhora da Conceição	100
Igreja de Santa Maria Maior	58
Igreja do Carmo	53
Igreja do Colégio	51
Island of Flowers	6
Isle of Eternal Spring	6
Isola di Lolegname	8

J

Jardim Botânico	62
Jardim de Loiros	63
Jardim de Santa Catarina	39
Jardim de São Francisco	33
Jardim do Mar	78
Jardim do Monte Palace	69
Jardim Orquídea	63
João Gonçalves Zarco	27,32
John Dos Passos	80

K

King João	137

L

Largo da Fonte	65
Largo do Município	100
Largo do Pelourinho	114
Largo do Phelps	53
Lavadas	22
Levada da Central da Ribeira da Janela	132
Levada da Serra do Faial	133
Levada do Furado	126
Levada dos Tornos	131
Levada do Caldeirão Verde	136
levadas	122
Lombada	80
Lota	101

M

Machico	100,105
Madalena do Mar	79
Madeiran Music Festival	24
Madeiran Wine Rally	25
Madeira Wine	34
Maps	124
Moinhos	96
Molhe da Pontinha	42
Monte	65
Monte Toboggans	68
Municipal Theatre	37
Museu da Baleia (Whaling Museum)	108
Museu da Cidade	52
Museu de Arte Contemporânea	58
Museu de Arte Sacra	50
Museu de Electricidade	57
Museu de Fotografia Vicentes	44
Museu do Bordada e do Artesanto	59
Museu do Vinho	52
Museu Franco	59
Museu Frederico de Freitas	47
Museum of Sacred Art	52
Museu Municipal	48

N

Nossa Senhora do Monte	65

P

Palheiro houses	85
Palheiros	91
Paso de Poiso	83
Patricio & Gouveia	59
Paúl da Sierra	76
Paúl do Mar	78
Pearl of the Atlantic	6
Pharmacies	149
Pico de Arieiro	83,129
Pico do Castelo	116
Pico do Facho	101
Pico dos Barcelos	72
Pico Ruivo	16,129,135
Pirates	29
Ponta da Calheta	115
Ponta da São Lourenço	128
Ponta de Garajau	95
Ponta de São Lourenço	104
Ponta do Pargo	77
Ponta do Sol	78,79
Ponte Delgada	86
Portela	108,117
Porto	115
Porto da Cruz	108
Porto Moniz	76,88
Porto Santo	27,110
Portuguese	12
Praça da Autonomia	56
Praça do Município	50
Prazeres	78

Q

Queimadas	85
Quinta Boa Vista	63
Quinta das Cruzes	43,45
Quinta do Palheiro Ferreiro (Blandy's Garden)	64
Quinta Magnólia	41
Quinta Splendida	96
Quinta Vigia	39

R

Rabaçal	77,130
Restaurants	142
Ribeira Brava	79,80
Ribeira da Janela	88
Ribeiro Frio	84
Ribeiro Frio: Levada do Furado	137
Rua da Carreira	43
Rua da Conceição	53
Rua dos Ferreiros	49
Rua João Tavira	48

Index

S

Santa	89
Santa Cruz	95,96
Santana	85
Santana to São Jorge	134
Santo da Serra	105
São Jorge	86
São Lourenço	104
São Vicente	86,90
Seixa	188
Selvagens	117
Serra de Água	90
Sisi	40
Sister Maria Clementina	44
Spain	11

T

Terras de Aventura & Turismo	139
Terreiro da Luta	69
The Desertas Islands	117
The Madeira Wine Company	33

V

| Vila Baleira | 114 |

W

| Walks | 122 |
| wicker toboggans | 69 |

Z

| Zarco | 42 |

Published in the UK by
Landmark Publishing Ltd,
Ashbourne Hall, Cokayne Ave, Ashbourne, Derbyshire DE6 1EJ England
Tel: (01335) 347349 Fax: (01335) 347303 e-mail: landmark@clara.net

2nd Edition
ISBN 13: 978 1 84306 326 1
ISBN: 1 84306 326 3

© Richard Sale 2007

The right of Colin Macdonald as author of this work has been asserted by him in accordance with the Copyright, Design and Patents Act, 1993. All rights reserved. No part of this publication may be reproduced, stored in a retrieval system or transmitted in any form or by any means, electronic, mechanical, photocopying, recording or otherwise without the prior permission of Landmark Publishing Ltd. British Library Cataloguing in Publication Data: a catalogue record for this book is available from the British Library.

Print: Cromwell Press, Trowbridge
Design & Cartography: Michelle Hunt

Front cover: Cortejo Flower Festival
Back cover, top: Funchal
Back cover, bottom: Porto Santo

Photograph acknowledgements
Richard Sale:
30 T & B,35,39, B Left & B Right,43,51,66 T & B,67.102,122,126 T Left & T Right,127

Direcção Regional Turismo Madeira:
Front Cover,6,11 T & B, 10 T & B,14 T & B,15,18,19 T & B,26,31,39 T,55,58,62,71,74,79 T & B,82,87 T & B,91,94,98,99,110,114,115,126 B

DISCLAIMER
While every care has been taken to ensure that the information in this book is as accurate as possible at the time of publication, the publishers and authors accept no responsibility for any loss, injury or inconvenience sustained by anyone using this book.